PERRY-MANSFIELD
PERFORMING ARTS SCHOOL & CAMP

PERRY-MANSFIELD
PERFORMING ARTS SCHOOL & CAMP

A History of Art in Nature

Thank you so much for sharing your story! & your adventures!
Dagny McKinley

Dagny McKinley

THE
History
PRESS

Published by The History Press
Charleston, SC
www.historypress.net

First published 2017

Manufactured in the United States

ISBN 9781625859273

Library of Congress Control Number: 20179344932

Art is born of nature.
—Charlotte Perry

I hear that mountains are not considered permanently any more—just temporary properties that hump around and nudge and shove each other into new arrangements every million years or so. The Rockies especially are young upstarts. So glad I passed their way.
—Postcard from Portia to Charlotte

This book is dedicated to Rusty DeLucia and T. Ray Faulkner—the second generation of Perry-Mansfield.

To the generations that follow, may you feel the spirit of the wild and the swirling leaves of creativity in your souls as you step foot onto these sacred grounds.

CONTENTS

ACKNOWLEDGEMENTS

This book could not have been written without the help of so many people. A huge thank-you to Perry-Mansfield Performing Arts School and Camp for giving me access to its archives. Much gratitude to the Steamboat Springs Arts Council and its Give Creativity a Shot Re-Grant Program for awarding me a grant to continue working on this book.

Thank you to the following institutions: Colorado Historic Newspapers Collection, Denver Public Library, History Colorado, New York Library for the Performing Arts, Dorothy and Lewis B. Cullman Center, Off the Beaten Path Bookstore, Rollins Academy and Smith College.

Thanks to Lucile Bogue for the extensive interviews she conducted and preserved while working on her book *Dancers on Horseback*. Additional thanks to Will Carpenter, Chris Compton, Tammy Dyke-Compton, Rusty DeLucia, Nancy Engelken, T. Ray Faulkner, Noel Hefty, Kim Keith, Wendy Kowynia, Joan Lazarus, Karolynn Lestrud, Ann Perry, Ditty Perry, Ken Perry, Leda Reed, Bruce Roach, Jim Steinberg, Lee Tillotson, Kay Uemura, Ingrid Wekerly, Bob Weiss, Holly Williams and Belle Zars.

My love and appreciation to my father for a place to work and all the support in the world, to my sister for the wine and dinners and taking care of me, to Tom Thurston for loving me and to Alma Rose for reminding me every day what joy is.

FOREWORDS

Perry Mansfield is one-of-a-kind, inspirational, spiritual and historical. The pioneers of modern dance helped to grow this program, and it is not an exaggeration to say that dance would not be where it is today without Perry-Mansfield. It is a part of our dance heritage—where we as dancers come from. There is not another place on earth quite like it. It is life changing. It feeds the soul, rejuvenates the spirit and educates and challenges the artist. Perry-Mansfield is that rare place where you can develop your technique and artistry while you connect with nature, friends and history. It's what life is about!

Perry-Mansfield provides the artist-student with an opportunity to turn potential into skill through concentrated effort, while allowing the freedom to explore and discover. The history of this place seeps into your soul and changes who you are forever. It connects us to our dancing roots. It gives dancers a space where they focus only on themselves and their art form, while simultaneously diving into new friendships that will last a lifetime. At Perry-Mansfield, you escape the rest of the world. With no distractions (no television, no cellphones, no Internet), all you have is you—your mind, heart and soul, to take you on the journey, free to explore, learn and challenge your previous notions and ideas. Immersed in the beautiful mountains of Colorado, you are pushed as an artist to study more than your own craft. The dancers take acting, the actors take dance and all take visual art, as well as creative writing. All of these art forms support one another and work to create a complete artist. And that is our ultimate goal.

—Tammy Dyke-Compton and Christopher Compton

Perry-Mansfield is, and shall always be, my home. From that magical moment in the summer of 1955, when I first set my wide, astonished eyes on the Rocky Mountains...peering through the dusty windows of an old diesel passenger train on my way to Steamboat...I knew that this is where my soul lives!

Dagny McKinley's history of my beloved home has brought back childhood memories that I'll cherish forever! In fact, I remember remarking, that summer, that the stork had surely made a grave mistake when it dropped me in New York City!

Kingo, Helen, Portia, Perry-Mansfield and Steamboat Springs have shaped and molded who I am today. I am so grateful that Dagny's words have brought those wonderful years back to me so vividly!

—Rusty DeLucia

INTRODUCTION

Perry-Mansfield Performing Arts School and Camp is the oldest continually running performing arts camp in the United States. The camp was founded on the principles that an exploration of the arts in a natural setting would create new inspiration for art as well as allow for collaboration between artistic disciplines while challenging campers physically, artistically and emotionally. Charlotte (Kingo) Perry and Portia Mansfield spent their lives "lifting" people, encouraging others to follow their dreams no matter how impossible they appeared. They worked tirelessly, pursuing their passions until the day they died. They never looked back on life. They were too busy looking forward.[1]

1887

On November 19, 1887, Portia Mansfield Swett was born in Chicago, Illinois, to Myra Swett and Edward R. Swett. Portia's father worked in hotel management, and his career took the family from Chicago to Michigan, Florida and New York City. When Portia was six, her sister, Margery "Petite" Swett, was born. As children, they explored the woods and wilderness around them, transforming the woods into worlds spawned from their imaginations. As adults, they traveled the world. At an early age, Portia and her family moved to a dark hotel in a poor part of town. To escape the hotel, Portia often snuck into a theater across the street, where *Uncle Tom's Cabin* was being rehearsed. The tension, beauty, pain and sacrifice of the performance made a lasting impression on her.[2]

From there, her father moved to a position with the Del Prado Hotel in Chicago. This is where Portia gave her first dance performances—to boarders in the lobby, at least until one of the boarders asked her to sit on his lap. From Chicago, the family moved north to Michigan's Lake Harbor Hotel and real winters. When she turned twelve, the family headed to Florida. During a train delay, the Swetts saw a circus parade through the window. A young woman jumped on the back of a horse and began dancing. Seeing her, Portia thought, "At last! I've found something I want to be." She declared, "I'm going to be a dancer on a horse in a circus."[3]

At fourteen, Portia finally took to the stage to dance with the Floradora Sextets under the tutelage of a family friend, Kirk Clugston. Clugston stayed with the Swetts when they moved to the Cumberland Hotel in New York. Portia and Clugston were given theater tickets when her parents couldn't make the shows. They held hands as they walked to the Keith and Orpheum Theaters to watch some of the top performers of their time.

In New York, Portia attended private school, where she was required to memorize a poem each day. Her English teacher rekindled a love of learning in her and encouraged her to attend Smith College for Women. She was accepted. She said her goodbye to Clugston and returned to Lake Harbor, Michigan, with her family the summer before she was to attend Smith College. On the day of her departure, her father drove her to the train in their horse and buggy. He said his farewells and told her to be a good girl. Two weeks later, he passed away from an attack of thrombosis. Swett left the family very little money, but he did leave Portia with a spirit of adventure.[4] After her father passed, Portia's education at Smith took on new importance, as she would have to work after graduation, which was not common for women of social standing at that time.

1889

Charlotte Louise Perry was born on December 21, 1889, in Denver, Colorado, to Samuel Perry and Lottie Matson Perry. After Sam and Lottie married, they moved from Chicago to Denver to help ease Lottie's severe asthma. The couple had three children, of whom Charlotte was the youngest. Marjorie Perry was the eldest and Robert Perry, also known as Robin or Bobby, the middle child.

Sam Perry was eventually promoted to president of the Denver Tramway Company. His business dealings and friendship with David Moffat were instrumental in bringing the Moffat railroad from Denver through Oak Creek and the Perry coal mines and on to Steamboat Springs, Colorado, where Perry-Mansfield Performing Arts School and Camp (P-M) was later established. Perry's business dealings in mining earned his family a fortune and a prominent place in Denver society.

In the Perry family, the girls were expected to do the same chores as their brother, so they learned how to gather and chop wood and milk cows. The value of hard work stuck with Charlotte throughout her life, as did the excitement that came from the great outdoors. For fun, Sam Perry took his children camping. When Charlotte was four, Sam Perry packed the family up for a trip to the mountains north of Denver. As they got close, Charlotte exclaimed, "Papa, we're going to bump into them."[5]

Just as Charlotte was fascinated with the outdoors at a young age, the theater also captured her imagination. When asked by a local paper what she wanted to be when she grew up, she responded,

> *I would like to be an actress because I like to sing and play and I am a fairy and a robber and a ghost or goblin and live in caves, or I would like to play George Washington and paint and powder my hair white and I would like to be leader of the American army and ride on a white horse and I like to wear dresses trimmed with gold or beautiful velvet trousers. This is the reason I would like to be an actress.*[6]

Her father can be credited with encouraging Charlotte's interest in theater, despite his admonitions that theater was for immoral women. Avoiding the opera with his wife one night, Sam took Charlotte to a performance of *Davy Crockett* at the Curtis Theatre. Being so close to the actors and seeing the story brought to life made a deep impression on Charlotte.

In the summers, Charlotte performed at Elitch Gardens' children's theater program. She attended the Wolcott School, now known as the Kent School, during her high school years. Mrs. Charles Vail, Charlotte's teacher, offered to direct her and the other neighborhood children in a performance of *Robin Hood*. Sam Perry signed Charlotte up for classes with a martial arts instructor so Charlotte could learn to use a stave properly. When the production needed green vests, Charlotte cut the green felt from her father's pool table. The jackets came out perfectly; her father's reaction remained in line with his excitable nature.[7]

After graduating high school, Charlotte followed in her sister's footsteps and attended Smith College.

1906

Portia began her education at Smith College. Her red hair, which hung to her waist, quickly earned a reputation of its own. Although she found herself bored with the formalities of college, she filled every spare moment. To earn money to help pay tuition, she knitted Irish lace collars for two dollars each, which was a good sum of money at that time. She tutored in tennis, philosophy and psychology. She joined the philosophical club, tennis team and equestrian program, did gymnastics and played wing for the hockey team. She founded a mandolin club that held concerts at other colleges. Each week, she recorded thirty-six hours of physical activity. On weekends, she taught dance at a mental institute nearby.

Portia was instrumental in organizing dance classes at Smith. At that time, there were no dedicated dance teachers. Her style of dance, modeled after Isadora Duncan, captured the hearts of faculty and students alike. She was the lead in any dance performance and was an excellent actress. In dance class, she and other students studied the Gilbert method of dance. There was no musical accompaniment, not even a stick to keep the beat. Girls dressed in heavy serge bloomers with four yards of material on each leg. Over the bloomers was a circular woolen skirt that came to just below the knee. A serge waist was also worn with long black cotton-ribbed stockings. Dancing consisted of holding the skirt between the thumb and middle finger of each hand, keeping a curved line from shoulder to fingertip. This position was held for the entire hour-long dance lesson. "Steps were basic: step, step, point the toe, back, back, back, point your toe and then to the side, point your toe. Finally, they were taught to turn around once, and all the girls found that very exciting. An occasional stilted pirouette and a little leap from one foot to the other were sometimes inserted."[8]

She also learned the Delsarte method of dance. Delsarte introduced the idea that body gestures communicated much more than words about the emotional state of a person. He believed the physical of the body corresponded to the trunk and arms, the emotional to the neck and the mental to the head.[9] His method was incorporated into modern dance through Ted Shawn and Doris Humphrey and later into Portia's "Correctives," exercises to help dancers with posture.

When Portia neared graduation, her instructor, Miss Berensen, encouraged her to continue her dance studies with Louis H. Chalif, the Russian dancer, at his studio in New York. Portia's dance career at Smith culminated in a performance on the lawn in front of faculty and students. Portia discarded her shoes, heavy bloomers and all things restrictive and danced barefoot in a gauzy dress. One of her teachers, Miss Peck, exclaimed, "Portia dances like a falling star."[10]

1907

In 1907, Charlotte began her Smith College education. "She loved everything that brought her in touch with the sights and smells and shapes of natural things. She seemed to have a sixth sense, like animals, and smelled and breathed and reacted to everything out of doors. If you had seen her at this time, you might have thought she was a person who had gone to college to take 'a course in New England,' but who only dropped in to classrooms as a secondary interest."[11] Charlotte was drawn to the arts. She took violin lessons and played in the orchestra until an infection in her shoulder prevented her from continuing. She joined the Alpha, Smith's dramatic society, and was chosen for the part of Graciano in *The Merchant of Venice* the year she graduated.

At Smith, Charlotte cut her hair short and got a perm. Her friends called her Carlo Kinks, which was later shortened to Kinko, then Kingo, a nickname she carried for life.

In her English class, Charlotte Perry met Helen Smith. Smith was shy but extremely intelligent. Her class assignment, "Observations from the Third Row Back," was singled out as what Charlotte called "a work of genius." The women's friendship lasted a lifetime, and as the years passed, Helen Smith became the dash in Perry-Mansfield. She was the glue that held Charlotte and Portia's friendship and working relationship together.

1910

Portia graduated from Smith in 1910. She visited Europe with her mother, sister and college friend, where they climbed mountains and explored small villages. This first adventure overseas aroused a wanderlust in Portia, who would later visit cultures around the world to learn from them and bring back new inspiration for her dances.

When she returned to New York, she began training at the Louis H. Chalif Normal School of Dancing. Two weeks into her classes, the students were asked to give a performance. Portia broke tradition and stepped onto the stage in a dark navy blue silk dress with a shock of yellow silk around her waist, instead of the preferred black dress. She also stepped out of the traditional five dance positions. While her classmates were debating whether her performance was real dance, Chalif offered her a job teaching dance to New York's schoolchildren for $1.50 a day.

For her first class, five hundred shining young faces greeted Portia on the piers. She had a twenty-piece band to compete with the noise of traffic, boats passing and other commotion. No one could hear a thing she said, so she took a child's hand and began basic dance steps. Steamers passing by tooted their approval. To save money to help support her mother and sister, she walked two miles each way to class instead of taking a cab.[12]

During Portia's second summer with Chalif, she was offered a job in Omaha, Nebraska, where she taught etiquette, curtseying and ballroom dances. When she wanted to teach her students a different style of dance and no one was interested, she offered gypsy and folk dancing to a few girls for free. They gave a performance at the next cotillion, and after that, her classes were full. She is believed to be the first person to take gypsy and folk dance west of the Mississippi.

In Omaha, Portia, who was enamored with modern dance, was inspired when she saw ballet dancer Anna Pavlova perform. Portia thought the manner with which Pavlova infused dance with dramatic acting was impeccable and realized the importance of the technical training of ballet. During her time in Omaha, Portia signed up for classes at the Brandeis School of Acting with Lillian Fitch in order to improve her own dramatic abilities.

1911

During both Portia's and Charlotte's years at Smith, President Seelye gave frequent lecture in which he would exhort his audience, "Are you a leaner or a lifter? You can accomplish important acts. You can change society. You must not wait for somebody else to do it."[13] His words made a huge impression on Charlotte and Portia, and they shaped their attitude to life around those words.

The year of Charlotte's graduation, Portia returned for her alumni reunion. The women first met two days after Charlotte's commencement at a house party. Their shared interests made them fast friends. For their first outing together, Portia picked up Charlotte in a friend's horse-drawn carriage. They rode around the countryside. On their return, Charlotte reported to a mutual friend, "Portia's a darling girl, but she's awfully absentminded."[14] That night, Portia knocked on Charlotte's window at 3:00 a.m. and asked her to climb to the top of Mount Tom, the southernmost and tallest peak in the Mount Tom range. It was here that Charlotte invited Portia to a bear hunt in Colorado that fall.

Charlotte graduated from Smith with a bachelor of arts degree in English literature and botany. "In the spring of 1911 when I graduated, Helen asked me where I was going in the summer. I said, 'Why home of course.' She said, 'I have a job.'" Charlotte thought of that with wonderment, as she was expected to come home and "come out" (with a debutante ball). "The girls all came out and I refused to," Charlotte said. "I thought it was a stupid thing and an unjustified expense."[15]

In the fall of 1911, Portia arrived in Denver to visit Charlotte. She stayed at the Perry house, where Mrs. Perry asked her to perform under the moonlight in her dancing shift for friends of the Perrys. Those who saw her performance were some of the most influential society women of the day, including Annie Dickinson Brown, who would later offer her summer lodge as a home for the first year of Rocky Mountain Dancing Camp. As the Victrola played, Portia danced barefoot, exciting those in attendance as well as those peeping over the fence.[16]

From Denver, they traveled to Rifle, Colorado, for the bear hunt. The hunt was successful, with Sam, Marjorie, Bob and Charlotte all taking a bear. Charlotte, however, was the only one affected by the experience. She vowed that day to never shoot another bear again. During this trip, Portia and Charlotte hatched their plans to start a dance camp in the mountains, away from the hot, sticky summers of the big cities. The only obstacle they had was how to earn money to make their camp a reality.

Charlotte Perry (*left*) and Portia Mansfield dance in the style of Isadora Duncan. *Perry-Mansfield Archives.*

Portia mused, "Kingo and I thought it would be great fun to have a summer cabin in the mountains....So that summer or the next, we decided to find a little spot and build a cabin. We decided we couldn't afford to just go up there for a weekend, we didn't want to, we'd get lazy. Then it occurred to us 'Why not take some of my dance students up into the mountains?' They would love it like we did.'"[17]

1912

More than once Charlotte approached her father about working, but he always said no. "Why did you give me an education if you didn't want me to use it?"[18] Charlotte challenged. Eventually, he allowed her to go to secretarial school. Afterward, he hired her as his secretary but gave her no work to do. Finally, he agreed that the next job that came her way she could take.

Serendipitously, Portia had moved to Chicago to work for a Miss Morgan teaching dance at Miss Morgan's Dramatic School. When Morgan needed a secretary, Kingo was the first person Portia contacted. Sam Perry let her go. In Chicago, Portia and Charlotte lived at Hull House, a settlement house designed to give an education to immigrant women and their children. On top of teaching at the settlement house—Portia in dance and Charlotte in basketball and Bible studies (her dramatizations of the Bible were considered scandalous)—the two worked full days and taught private dance lessons on the side. Portia also commuted between Omaha and Chicago twice a week on a sleeper train to continue teaching her former students. On top of her hectic schedule, Portia signed up for ballet classes with Andreas Pavley at his Chicago studio. When Pavley and Serge Oukrainsky established the Pavley-Oukrainsky Ballet Company, Portia was invited to join.

Brochure from the early years of Perry-Mansfield Performing Arts School & Camp. *Perry-Mansfield Archives.*

Charlotte was quickly promoted from secretary to drama teacher. In her spare time, she studied at the Art Institute of

Chicago under Jean Mannheim. On top of all their other commitments, Portia and Charlotte made time to travel to New York to take lessons from Irene and Vernon Castle. Inspired, they brought the fox trot and the hesitation waltz to the south side of Chicago, where they taught up and down the coast. They saved every last penny they had for their camp, which often meant they went without a good meal. "Some mornings on their way to teach they stopped in front of a bakery salivating over the cakes as the smell of warm fruit and bread wafted out the door. The two women would hold hands and close their eyes filling their bellies with their imaginations. 'Which one did you eat?' asked Portia. 'Don't bother me, I'm still on my apple pie,' Charlotte responded."[19]

Charlotte and Portia also traveled to Europe where, through the art they saw, Charlotte first started to understand groupings for the stage.

1913

The women continued to work in Chicago to earn money for their camp. Charlotte finally told her father she was going to start a summer camp with Portia. He threatened to disown her if she lost a single penny her first year. When Charlotte didn't back down, Sam arranged for a private car to transport students from Chicago to Denver.

1
THE EARLY YEARS

1914

Neither Portia nor Charlotte had ever visited or attended a camp before, but they were not daunted by the prospect of opening one. They named their camp Rocky Mountain Dancing Camp (RMDC):

> *It is to be deep in the heart of the Rocky Mountains, where the rushing streams flow straight from the snowy peaks of the Great Divide, and the wind blows fresh through the forests of dense pine and spruce. Here life is free, simple, and sweet. For perfect expression in dancing, music or any creative art, freedom of the body, and of the spirit, is necessary. Life in the great silence of the stern white peaks is healthful and free, it recreates the body and the mind in simplicity and beauty.*[20]

The first year of camp was held at Lake Eldora at Dixie Lodge, Annie Dickinson Brown's palatial summer retreat. The lodge boasted screened-in porches, two lakes, a boathouse and a gazebo all done in an oriental design.[21]

Dance camp started on July 15, with fifteen students recruited from Portia's classes in Chicago and Omaha, as well as classmates from Smith College and Denver socialites. Some students came with their mothers, who cooked or played piano in exchange for board for their daughters.

While the lodge was elaborate, the experience was rugged, with dance, drama and sleeping arrangements taking place on screened-in porches. The

Portia Mansfield and Charlotte Perry during their first year of camp in Eldora, Colorado, in 1913. *Perry-Mansfield Archives.*

high altitude, at approximately nine thousand feet, made dancing difficult for some students, as did the thunder and lightning storms that crashed in every afternoon for two hours. The noise was so overwhelming that everything stopped until the storms passed.

Charlotte and Portia were the only instructors, yet the schedule of classes was intense.

> *The twittering of the birds every morning were answered by the dancers—it was early to bed and early to rise. In their flowing robes they danced until after the sun was up and then a plunge in the lake. Then a change to one piece knickerbockers and bloomers. A light luncheon, and then the strenuous mountain climbing, calisthenics and aesthetic interpretation of some old Greek play in a pine-walled natural theater, a wholesome dinner, a little classical music, then to bed.[22]*

For dinner, campers dressed in their finest clothes, a tradition that was held at camp until Charlotte and Portia sold P-M in 1963. Not long after the opening of camp, a man hiking in the hills spotted the girls. Shortly afterward, a picture of the dancers in filmy dresses made the Denver papers with the headline "Shades of Zebulon Pike! Scantily-Clad Girls Will Dance on Colorado Peaks."[23] Soon the hillside across from camp was spotted with men with spyglasses hoping for a glimpse of the nymphs dancing. One man was brave enough to approach the gate seeking entrance. Charlotte, who had been teaching a wood-chopping class, answered the call with axe in hand, and the man quickly retreated.[24] At the end of camp, the women had earned a $200 profit. From then on, Sam Perry supported his daughter's efforts.

After their first year, they knew they needed to relocate camp for more privacy. They continued to work in Chicago during the winters. They took classes from a casket maker at the Lewis Institute in Chicago to learn how to build furniture that could be taken apart, laid flat and shipped across the country by train. Charlotte and Portia spent two seasons learning to make a birdhouse before they were finally given the freedom to try to make furniture. Neither the teacher nor the other men

Denver papers reported stories of nymphs dancing in the hills above Boulder, Colorado. *Perry-Mansfield Archives.*

in the class had any confidence in the ladies' building skills, but when they screwed in the last bolt of the chair they had designed, it stood. The men changed their tune and congratulated the two women. The furniture they built still stands at P-M today.

1915

Because of the Perry mining interests in Oak Creek, Colorado, Charlotte's brother offered to help find a location for RMDC nearby. Initially, they considered a site near Crosho Lake in what is today the Flat Tops wilderness; however, severe weather patterns in the area quickly discouraged that notion.

They eventually purchased fifteen acres of land with a homesteader's cabin on it from F.A. Metcalf in Strawberry Park, near the town of Steamboat Springs. The site—purchased for $200—was away from prying eyes. "We called it a camp because we and our students would live under primitive conditions and would swim and ride and explore the mountain country,"[25] Charlotte later recalled.

For transportation, Bobby Perry gave the ladies a mule that was considered too vicious for work at the mines. "Bobby told us to give him a new name and genuine affection. We named him Tango and treated him with trust, treatment which has often proved useful to us since,"[26] said Charlotte.

To build the camp, they hired miners from the Perry mines. Not long after they started, the men threatened to walk off the job because of the food. The ladies had been feeding them the best French recipes they could find. When Charlotte called her brother, he said, "No wonder they're ready to quit. You've got to cover everything in gravy and lard." Charlotte did as her brother instructed. As a result, Main Lodge, a forty- by fifty-foot structure used for dance classes and plays, and six wooden cabins with canvas tops on the ridge above Soda Creek were completed just in time for camp to open.[27] The living room of Cabeen, the original cabin, served as a dining room, recreation and rehearsal hall.

Water came from a spring 150 feet down the ridge and had to be pumped up with a hand crank to a large tank on the ridge. It was then piped to the kitchen.[28] Candles and kerosene lamps served as the only light on campus. "At supper, when all the candles were lighted, camp took on a magical and unearthly glow," remembered Charlotte.[29]

Portia Mansfield and Charlotte Perry helped build camp. *Perry-Mansfield Archives.*

During those first years in Steamboat, Charlotte and Portia were referred to as "the mad ladies." Reports of nudity abounded. Ranchers warned their wives not to step foot on camp property, as "those ladies" were believed to be "in cahoots with the devil." One woman even threatened to run them out of town.[30] Supplies were left at the entrance to camp by the creek. In order to bring supplies into camp, because there was no road at the time, Charlotte and Portia had to either strap supplies onto their backs or bring down Tango and the cart.

From the earliest days, family was enlisted to help run camp. Marjorie Perry, Charlotte's sister, headed the riding program. Margery Mansfield, Portia's sister and a poetess, assisted in creative writing and wrote one of her most recognized poems at camp. Myra Swett, Portia's mother, helped sew costumes for many years until her eyes finally failed her. Sam Perry stepped in when necessary to help close camp. He also arranged for a special Pullman private car on the train to deliver students to camp.

Cooks were hired to help and were critical to the success of camp. America, from Lincoln, Nebraska, was the first cook, followed by her friends Peeler and Poky. All three women stayed until 1963, when P-M was sold to Stephens College. Eventually, Lorene Workman was hired to help as well and stayed twenty-two years, making the transition between Perry-Mansfield and Stephens College's ownership.

Isadora Duncan strongly influenced modern dance at camp. Girls were taught to celebrate the beauty of their bodies. *Perry-Mansfield Archives.*

Above: During the first years of Rocky Mountain Dance Camp, Charlotte and Portia's sisters were integral parts of the faculty. *From left to right*: Margery Mansfield, Portia Mansfield, Charlotte Perry and Marjorie Perry. *Perry-Mansfield Archives.*

Below: America (*left*), Poky (*center*) and Peeler, camp's beloved cooks. *Perry-Mansfield Archives.*

Enrollment grew to twenty girls the second year of camp. Staff helped put in a road, cut wood for fires, cleared underbrush and created walkways. Classes involved learning how to chop wood, clear trails, make curtains, stain walls and floors, dance, act and ride horseback.[31] "This was doubtless good for the arts in the long run. Isben's and Synge's and Lorca's characters fulfill their destinies close to earth, sea and weather, and the actors and directors who step into their mired and worn shoes need to have lived close to the out-of-doors and been subject to its alternating violence and peace."[32]

In those first years, Portia was camp director while Charlotte was the manager. Swimming and horseback riding were integral components of the program. Swimming instruction and competitions were held at the bathhouse in town, where hot springs naturally heated the pools. The equestrian program was touted as

A Most Unusual and Complete Department Under the Direction of Marjorie Perry Assisted by Frances Hartsook

A horse and a night on a mountain can teach more of the beauty and majesty of nature than can many, many books. Much of the most beautiful country in the Rocky Mountains is inaccessible except on horseback. Only on horses can one climb up the dark, rocky canyons to the clear lakes that lie like blue jewels in the grassy meadow at the tops of the mountains. Here the pines are thick and fragrant and hundreds of marsh marigolds sparkle like little stars in the green grass.[33]

Monday was "Trip Day," when campers rode up into the hills to find wild raspberries, choke-cherries, mushrooms and waterfalls. Excursions included climbing up over ten thousand feet to timberline lakes. Sometimes, campers were awakened at 3:00 a.m. for a ride through the town of Steamboat under the stars to the Steamboat Quarry high above town. There they ate breakfast as the sun rose. Charlotte cooked eggs any way you wanted them, songs were sung and stunts indulged in. Because the days were so full, Charlotte and Portia worked by lantern or moonlight to take care of sick horses or plant potatoes and beans.[34]

At the end of the second year of camp, one of the students' fathers showed up with a Cinematographe motion picture camera. The cameras took photographs and and printed and projected films. Portia, a born photographer, was immediately intrigued. She purchased a film camera for herself and began documenting dance, theater and wilderness trips at camp.

Girls pack their horses for an overnight trip. *Perry-Mansfield Archives.*

Her films were later the only record of many early modern dances and were rented to educational institutions across the country and around the world. Her love of film was so great that even in her later years, Portia could be found asleep in bed with strips of film surrounding her.

1916

Camp was divided into two classes, Juniors and Seniors, with six weeks of study for each group. Students who wanted to attend and couldn't afford to do so were given scholarships in exchange for work. This helped cut the camp's cost by not having to hire as many full-time employees. When they had a student who wasn't doing a job well, Portia would say something like, "We feel that you would be much better as the person in charge of cleaning stables. We need to elevate you to that job." In that way, she was able to change and elevate people so they worked harder and so they never felt like they were failures.[35]

A stagecoach transported campers during the early years of camp. *Perry-Mansfield Archives.*

The camp program that year included

Grecian dances, technique of Russian dances, National dances (Russian, Grecian, Bohemian), interpretive dances and folk and rhythmic dances. Afternoons were given over to riding, bathing, climbing and general recreation. At the completion of the term the senior class was given diplomas. No dance classes were held Saturdays or Sundays. Saturday was set aside for rides, excursions and camping trips. Sunday was rest day.[36]

At the end of the year, when Charlotte and Portia went to the bank to take out their savings, they found out they owed the clerk twenty-nine dollars.[37] Fortunately, Sam Perry's threat to disinherit his daughter only applied to their first year of camp.

1917

Portia joined the American Camping Association, at the time called the Camp Directors Association of America, in order to learn how to better the summer experience for her campers, as well as to comply with national standards for safety and sanitation at camp.

Charlotte and Marjorie purchased ten additional acres of land on the east side of camp to accommodate increased attendance. To enhance camp, a cement tennis court was poured, which later became the main stage for Portia's photographs of dancers. Townspeople said the tennis court used more cement than the building of a house. This extravagance only egged on the opposition of the locals, who had a hard time understanding the purpose of a camp for the arts. That was at least until the local newspaper, the *Routt County Sentinel*, reviewed one of the camp's dance performances as tasteful, with dancers striving only to attain beauty and grace.

Because of World War I, fuel rations were instituted. As a way of giving to those in need, RMDC performers took a train to Denver to perform for the Fatherless Children of France. At the end of the show, a musician played the bagpipes down the aisle and into the street like the pied piper as the audience followed.

Tents with canvas awnings served as housing for the first years of camp. Every aspect of camp integrated nature into daily life. *Perry-Mansfield Archives.*

By the end of the summer, the future of the world felt so uncertain that the ladies declared Christmas in August as a way of celebrating friends and loved ones. A feast of steak, potatoes and vegetables was served while handmade gifts were exchanged. Christmas at the end of summer became a tradition that carried on through the years at camp, always with handcrafted gifts.

1918

To continue to entice students during the war years, the summer camp program expanded to include target practice, military drills, gardening, French language classes, Red Cross work, swimming, water sports, mountain climbing, horseback riding and, of course, dance.[38] The dance teacher for toe work was Franchelli of the Pavley-Oukrainsky Ballet Company and formerly a soloist with the Grand Opera in Vienna.[39] Margaret Bracken of New York instructed special courses in swimming, water sports and tennis.[40]

Counselors were schooled to help their campers become more independent and take responsibility for their actions while supervising them mentally and physically. They encouraged campers by putting campers' ideas into action whenever possible. For counselors, the three Fs were guiding principles: "be friendly, fair and firm and never say 'No' until you are sure it's the only answer."[41]

1919

Portia spent a portion of the winters recruiting students for camp by traveling across the country and giving presentations at prestigious schools and interviews to newspapers. The *St. Louis Dispatch* quoted Portia:

You may tell a woman to go forth and flit like a butterfly, but she cannot do that all at once unless she is possessed of all the qualities of a butterfly. With good solid Russian technique, though, and with conscientious study and practice, she can gain such command of her muscles that she can eventually give the semblance of a butterfly. "While I was in college I possessed none of the characteristics of a butterfly. I did not dance at all until I was out of college." She did not need to say, "and look at me now,"

Interior of the Main Lodge. *Perry-Mansfield Archives.*

for I had seen her direct aerial movements with a body seemingly boneless and light as thistle down, yet now she was no more out of breath than a bird after its flight, and she was radiantly calm and placid as a May morning.…She can out-do many a soldier in tests of physical endurance, I venture to say, and without the sacrifice of all that is sweetly feminine, for her endurance is manifested in dancing, the most grace-producing, as well as muscle-developing exercise for women. And she is a modest, maidenly personality with the diffidence and the low voice, considered such excellent things in woman.

Her efforts paid off, and by 1919, Rocky Mountain Dancing Camp had sixty campers and staff in attendance, with campers from Boston, Chicago, St. Louis, Omaha, Lincoln and Denver.[42] At this time, the camp officially carried two separate departments, one a professional school of dance and the other a recreation camp.[43] The recreation camp was said to bring in much-needed money to help fund the dance school.

While RMDC had made some inroads with the locals, it still hadn't been able to showcase its activities to a wide audience. All that changed when Ferry Carpenter, a good friend of Charlotte's brother, invited RMDC to his ranch north of Hayden to give a demonstration of dance at his annual party. Carpenter graduated from Princeton before moving to Hayden, Colorado, where he served as an attorney and became a rancher. Over six hundred guests arrived in autos, buggies and wagons and by horseback. Carpenter recalled the evening for the movie *A Divine Madness*, directed by Len Aitken:

> *The large front porch of the house had been extended several feet, making a new dancing platform, and this was prettily lighted by Japanese lanterns. There were colored lights in the yard, and spot lights from many of the autos completed a brilliant illumination, while a big campfire added to the pretty effect of the decorations. A fountain in the yard, supplied with water from a spring on the nearby mountain, was beautiful with the light of the campfire upon it. The dancers, Misses Charlotte and Marjorie Perry, Portia Swett, Pleasant Holyoke, Hazel O'Connor and Helen Weiffenbach, with music by Flavia Waters, began to dance.*
>
> *As they were giving their performance with scarves, each time a scarf was pulled away from a body or face, the cowboys yelled Wooooahhh, like they would do to round up their cattle. So impressed was everyone there the women from Perry-Mansfield soon found themselves learning dances from the ranchers, which they added their own flavor to.*[44]

The dancing went on into the wee small hours of the morning.

1920

The year 1920 saw several additions to camp. A new outdoor studio for dancing was constructed with a stage at one end and a kitchen at the other. To help increase revenue, Club Camp for Adults was added to the summer program:

> *The club camp is conducted exclusively for adults, both men and women. The camp is situated in a secluded section, on the eastern slope of Strawberry Ridge, facing an extensive view across valley and mountain to the snow-capped peaks of the Divide.*
>
> *A hostess looks after the comfort of all campers. Breakfast is served on the terrace or before the fire. Those who prefer may have breakfast in bed. For other meals the campers usually go to the Main Lodge. Twice a week supper is served at the Club Camp.*

Members of this unit may participate in any of the sports, classes and activities of the camps and the Theatre Arts School. A camp car is available twice daily to take them to the hot baths and open air pool in Steamboat Springs.

Under the supervision of an experienced member of the riding department, they may take instruction in horsemanship or ride on the many cross country trails and dirt roads. Special trips are planned by automobile to the more remote places of interest in the surrounding area.[45]

The program was hugely successful, attracting the likes of the Rockefellers and Hollywood celebrities, but only lasted a few years. Charlotte and Portia felt too much focus was being placed on the adults and not enough on the campers.

From 1914 to 1920, the ladies returned to Chicago each fall to teach and study:

That year winter in Chicago was at its worst, streets so icy that our postman on his rounds had to tack from tree to tree and the wind…cut into our very hearts. We felt the winters were no longer for us so we notified our dance classes that we were taking a leave of absence, packed up our few belongings and sought out a place described to us by a former student as "just the place you'd expect to have your kind of a school, Carmel-by-the-Sea [California]." Disembarking in Carmel, the air was a blanket to keep us warm after the penetrating cold of Chicago. "What a miracle! What a perfume!" The Acacia trees were in bloom. Sandy streets ran down to the sea. A rocky, spicy shore full of cypresses and deep blue pools splashed up great fans of foam. At night, people walked soundlessly by the light of candle lanterns and the sweet smell of wood smoke came from every house.[46]

At the time, Carmel was still considered a small, poor neighborhood.[47] The ladies rented land from Frank Derendorf that had a low shingle house with fireplaces in the bedrooms, which opened east on a sunny terrace. Here they opened a winter school for dance. The *San Francisco Examiner* reported:

This winter the colony [Carmel] has been joined by three young society girls from Denver, who have established a camp there and who are among the interesting additions to the town folk. They are accomplished horsewomen and can break to saddle the wildest colt that roams the ranges; they can swim through the breakers far out to sea, but above all, they can dance. Every morning Miss Marjory, and Miss Charlotte Perry and Miss

Portia Swett, with their companions, all gowned in filmy draperies, dance barefooted along the beach.[48]

At the end of the season, they presented performances at the old Hotel Del Monte in Monterey, which received praise from local newspapers. When the dancing was done, students were invited to go on a four-day horseback trip camping at points along the coast and in the giant redwood forests.[49]

1921

By 1921, student enrollment had grown to sixty-five students. The program again expanded to include Girl Scout work, instruction in horsemanship, swimming, athletics, dramatics, designing, batiking, art-dyeing and pottery with Dorothea Denslow, who returned to camp for her second of what would be seven years of teaching sculpture. Instead of using clay, Denslow carved soap with her students. Cooks and hired hands joined in. Denslow went on to become the head of the Sculpture Center in New York.[50]

Art was an integral component of the Perry-Mansfield curriculum. *Perry-Mansfield Archives.*

Portia Mansfield dressed for a vaudeville performance. *Perry-Mansfield Archives.*

Art not only served as a creative outlet but also taught children a "feeling for proportion and line, to understand balanced work and the sense that useful things can and should be beautiful and beautiful things useful."[51]

Although dance had been the primary impetus for opening RMDC, Charlotte's love of theater ensured drama was also represented through classes that included pantomime, analysis of plays for production, commedia, makeup, scenery, lighting and costume design.

Each Monday, a few girls would be chosen by the dramatic coach to act out a short story or play that they had just been told about. The audience, knowing they had no rehearsal, had no expectations, so the student putting on the play would forget to be self-conscious. In the evenings, a great piece of literature or work of art might be discussed or music played.[52]

At the end of the summer, the top dance students were given an armband with a tiny triangle placed above winged shoes to represent dancing, designing and dramatics.[53]

At the end of camp each year, RMDC performers gave a demonstration in Denver at the Broadway Theater that included "Italian and Russian

41

methods of bar and toe work, dances of Oriental, Egyptian and Spanish origins, Greek plastique and a beautiful pantomime."[54] In 1921, Portia set up a tryout at the Orpheum Theatre for her top dancers, including Jeanne Fuller, Willette Allen, Frances Blaire Hartsook, Flavia Waters and Marjorie Leet.[55] The performance was a success, and an additional tryout was arranged for Ota Gygi, who had been violinist to the King of Spain, and Gygi's wife, Maryon Vadie, the foremost premier danseuse in America. Gygi invited the girls to dance for his vaudeville act. Jeanne Fuller, who first attended camp when she was eleven years old, was only fifteen when they auditioned. Portia put her in charge of the troupe. The highlight of the tour was playing the Palace Theatre in New York as the headline act.[56] After half a season, Jeanne Fuller left the company to go back to high school.

Given the notoriety of Portia's dancers, a friend of the family discreetly suggested she change her last name from "Swett" to something that would appear more appealing on billboards and posters. Portia enlisted the help of lawyer and friend Ferry Carpenter to change her name to Portia Mansfield, taking her mother's maiden name. Her dance troupe was called the Portia Mansfield Dancers, and the Rocky Mountain Dancing Camp formally became Perry-Mansfield Camp, or P-M. The board of directors consisted of Portia Mansfield, Charlotte Perry and Helen R. Smith. Smith, Charlotte's close friend from Smith College, began spending a portion of each summer at camp. With a PhD, Helen headed the Vocational Advisory Service in New York when she wasn't at camp. Smith's intelligence and ability to moderate situations fairly soon became a critical element for helping camp run smoothly.

2
VAUDEVILLE

1922

For the first time in nine years, students arrived at camp from Denver by automobile instead of train. That year, Portia received a letter from her cousin Virginia "Jinney" Mansfield saying that her father would not let her attend college and she didn't know what to do. Portia told her to "beg, borrow or steal the money" to come out to camp. If she did, Portia would take care of her from there. When Jinney's father left town on a business trip, she borrowed money from an uncle and left for Steamboat Springs. When her father found out what she had done, he disowned her. His anger was further compounded when Jinney went on to become one of the lead dancers in Portia's company, touring the vaudeville circuit. People believed that if you were performing vaudeville you were leading an immoral life. Only years later, when Jinney's mother insisted on seeing her perform, did Jinney's father realize the quality of the act and forgive her.[57]

Townspeople were also learning acceptance toward P-M. Horseback riding demonstrations and gymkhanas were opened to the public free of charge at the end of each summer. In 1922, M.D. Schaefermeyer brought a Magnavox and amplifier to play music from across the country in the open air at "distances of several hundred feet from the set. These demonstrations…will be a great novelty, as nothing of the kind has ever been heard before on the Western slope."[58]

The ladies' dance acts performed on the vaudeville circuit generated money to expand Perry-Mansfield Camp. *Copyright Bert's Studio, Perry-Mansfield Archives.*

Winter camp was moved from Carmel to Berkeley to increase exposure. Some of the most promising dancers from the summer were invited to Berkeley to continue their training. Informal performances were given on an invitation-only basis.[59] From these, the Perry-Mansfield Dancers were invited to try out for Grauman's Theatre in San Francisco. For the audition, Portia cut her famous red locks, which never grew back as long again. Their act was accepted, and they were given additional bookings at Grauman's Egyptian Theatre in Los Angeles. This launched their careers on the vaudeville circuit.

1923

When they returned to Steamboat following their winter performances, they worked on a new act. That fall, they approached New York agents and were turned down by just about every one. They were told that "no one wants to see an act with classical music and elegant sets—people want to be entertained."[60] Just as they were about to give up, Frederick Shipman offered to manage them based on their "Vivid and Colorful Dance Concert" embodying music visualizations of famous compositions. Their act was later compared to the Marion Morgan Dancers, and some even labeled them the Flo Ziegfeld of the vaudeville stage.[61]

The Portia Mansfield Dancers went on the road, and they would eventually tour on the Orpheum, Keith, Pantages, RKO and Gus and Son Circuits, with a stint on the Circuit of Broken Hearts. By 1923, the Portia Mansfield Dancers consisted of Jinney Mansfield and Helen Howell Parnell as lead dancers, along with Jeanne Fuller, Margaret Day Platt, Frances Hilliard, Alice Mickrey Volt, Kate Inglis Peters, Phyllis Unthank

Charlotte Perry dips Portia Mansfield during dance rehearsals. *Perry-Mansfield Archives.*

Underwood, Elizabeth Waters, Flavia Waters Champe, Frances Harstook and Mildred Wirt. Charlotte became one of the company's leading dancers while also serving as the group's general designer and technical director. Her work on vaudeville eventually allowed her membership into the Stage Designer's Union.

The reviews of their shows were often glowing:

> *Miss Mansfield's genius for dance composition supplemented by Miss Perry's high talents in costuming, lighting and scenic design bring forth creations that are unique among the contemporary art as expressed in the dance forums.*
>
> *The opening number is a visualization of "Pastorale" by Frederick Knight Logan, full of romantic beauty and causes our fancy to take flight to the days when Pan piped love and romance into the hearts of mortals.*
>
> *Then there is the "Fiesta De Seville" ballet, gorgeously costumed, vivid with the witchery and romance of Spain, fraught with the rhythm of castanets and the staccato of little red heels....*

A number which always arouses intense enthusiasm is "Saturnalia" portraying the celebration of the Roman Saturnalia. This dance affords an opportunity for amazing leaps, flying cartwheels, discus throwing, chariot racing, hurdling and wrestling.

The show ends with marvelous lighting effects and the moving of supple bodies under a gorgeous canopy of color.[62]

Despite the company's initial successes, there was still a strong contingency of Americans that felt dancing barefoot was immoral. When the tour reached White Plains, New York, they were given an ultimatum: no concert would be given unless the girls wore dance tights. Charlotte found a Smith (College) Club in White Plains, telephoned the president and explained the situation. The woman contacted the manager. Whatever she said worked, because they were allowed to go on. More than one venue threatened to cancel the concerts if the dancers didn't wear tights, but the only place they conceded to wearing stockings was in Oregon.[63]

Portia Mansfield's vaudeville acts were known for their professionalism and style. *Hartsook Photography; Perry-Mansfield Archives.*

Dancers leap with joy. *Perry-Mansfield Archives.*

Their Smith connections served them well on tour. At the end of one performance, a former classmate invited the ladies to fly in Orville Wright's plane. Of the flight, Charlotte wrote, "When we went to get into the airplane with Orville Wright, it was like a kite, with posts at each corner… no protection of any kind…and nothing to hang on to! We were thrilled to the core, blown to bits, cold as could be, with only light dress clothing and no coats of any kind."[64] Portia later went on to be one of the first people to travel around the world by airplane.

Summers were used for preparing new acts, sets and costumes. Early sets were made by dyeing white toweling an evening shade of blue and then sprinkling it with glue and silver bits intended to be stars. As they were making the set, "Charlotte's dog envisioned the contraption as one big play toy, rolling on and nipping at the material. When the material stuck to the dog, the dog ran down the street with Charlotte and the girls chasing after."[65]

A portion of each fall and winter was set aside for touring. Some tours had them performing four shows a day—two matinees in the afternoon and two shows at night—in order to keep the venues packed. Travel from one place to the next was by day coach or the occasional sleeper train.

One of the challenges of moving venue to venue was that the orchestra was usually local. Portia had to teach each new orchestra the music because she shortened certain numbers to fit her acts or made adjustments to the tempo. Always resourceful, Portia joined the Musicians Union, which she was able to do because she had been the director of the Mandolin Club at Smith College. "When the orchestra was good, however, and the stage large enough to move on, nothing mattered. We were all doing what we loved and on those occasions, when everything came to full tide rhythmically and emotionally—for that moment we were artists,"[66] wrote Charlotte of their experiences.

There were also challenges on the road, such as the time they had to cross a lake to perform for a Catholic congregation. The small theater with boiling pipes along the back and a lattice of fresh roses decorating the space wreaked havoc on the dancers. They decided against a backdrop, as a fire on stage would do nothing to enhance their performance. Their rehearsal consisted of avoiding collisions with one another, saving their scarves from the rose thorns and trying to avoid the boiling pipes, which was not always successful. Their hard work paid off when an old German wood carver with a big umbrella approached Charlotte and Portia after the second night's show to tell them that he had "modeled by memory for his granddaughter all he could remember of the flying movements and told her, 'Joost the valk of these girls is music!'" [67]

Often, just when everyone's spirits were low, circumstance provided much-needed comic relief. After being on the road for weeks, the dancers left the train straight for rehearsals. When they entered the building, the youngest dancer rushed over to a baby carriage "cooing with delight." She jumped back as quickly as she had leaned in. "A midget smoking a big black cigar is in there!" she reported. Encouraged by the response, the little person pinched her legs every time she passed him, much to her dismay.[68]

At the end of the performances, when there was time, a frying pan, coffee pot and food were gathered. The troupe took the streetcar to the end of the line at the edge of the city for an old-fashioned cookout, or "bat." All the time they toured they saved money to expand P-M. They lived off twenty-two cents for lunch, fifty cents for dinner and one dollar a night for lodging. Their savings paid for the building of Bucket, Mare's Nest, Nose Bag and Main Studio.

The Portia Mansfield Dancers toured across the United States and into Canada until film began to replace live acts. *From Virginia Mansfield's Archives, shared by Mary Ann Mansfield, wife of Malcolm B. Mansfield, nephew to Virginia Mansfield.*

1923

In 1923, the women set up their winter residence in New York. Portia and Charlotte taught rhythms, phrasing, ensemble, choreography, composition, Greek Plastique technique, interpretive body and arm work, aerial and floor technique, the foxtrot, Argentine tango, adagio studies, Spanish heel work, castanet playing, music appreciation, Russian and Italian technique, tap, soft shoe, buck and wing dancing, line work, musical comedy routines, limbering and stretching, beginning and advanced acrobatics and web work.[69] They taught at schools where they could also recruit students for summer camp.

1924

The notoriety of Perry-Mansfield Camp reached from coast to coast. Among the students in 1924 was Eleanor Bliss, who much later helped launch the Steamboat Springs Arts Council and was the recipient of the 1976 Governor's Award for Excellence in the Arts. During World War I, Bliss lived with her aunt, renowned dancer Eleanor T. Flinn, who financed lessons for Bliss with famous Russian ballet masters hoping she would take over the Flinn School of Dancing. As part of her training, she was sent to P-M. There she fell in love—not with dance, but with horses and the lifestyle Marjorie Perry lived. The two became lifelong companions.[70] While Bliss didn't return to camp, she did return to Steamboat each year to visit Marjorie and ride horses in the backcountry.

Marjorie Perry embraced every type of person and every type of animal. *Perry-Mansfield Archives.*

That summer, the riding program expanded its curriculum to include both English and western styles of riding to help increase interest and attendance. P-M became the first institution in the United States to offer both styles under one roof. In the same way, both ballet and modern dance were taught at camp, and students were required to learn both methods.

That year, the Official School of Theatre began and was headed by Lillian Fitch of the Brandeis School of Acting. Fitch directed in Hollywood and coached movie stars. Her classes included set design, lighting, staging, pantomime, analysis of plays, commedia, makeup, scenery, lighting and costume design. The final drama performance that year was an "Indian play" given on a hilltop situated against the night sky and lighted with campfires.[71]

After camp ended, Charlotte and Portia were on the road again. On Christmas Day, they found themselves in the worst dump in the two years they had been on the road. Christmas breakfast consisted of fried potatoes, cake and crackers. "So dismal," was Portia's note.[72]

After touring, Charlotte visited New Mexico, where she studied the "rhythm and grace of the aborigines."[73] The connection to and interest in Native American dances was strong, and for many years camp outings included visits to different Native American tribal lands to observe their dances.

1925

In 1925, the camp received electricity, and the Silver Spruce Theatre was built in order for the theater program to expand. During the vaudeville years, thirty-three new structures were added to camp, with each lodge or cottage having its own color scheme in both the furniture and interior decoration. Improvements included a modeling studio, a Little Theatre Workshop, a special studio for dancing, cabins for men, a camp hospital and a pen for jumping horses. One hundred campers attended P-M in 1925, approximately 30 percent more than in any other year.[74] With that many campers, safety measures were instituted:

- The first three days or week in this altitude guard against loss of breath. Do not run!
- Realize the importance of rest periods.
- Never drink water out of streams and rivers except in country above nine thousand feet.[75]

The rustic feel of camp was reflected in the song "Humoresque":

Humoresque
If you go to dancing camp, it's out of place to be a vamp.
Take off your lipstick and your powder, do (please do)
Let the wayward eyebrow grow and don't spring out in city clothes,
a dancer's charm lies in her sprightly toe (you know)
Your nose should shine cause it is natural,
leave your curlers in your satchel
and beware of incriminating goo.
So rouge your toesies if you must,
but keep your face clean if you bust
and leave cosmetics 'til you homeward go.[76]

With the popularity of P-M, the caliber of instructors increased. Among the teachers at camp in 1925 was Antoinette Perry (no relation to Charlotte). Perry was one of the few women directors of her time. After her passing, the Antoinette Perry Award was created, known today as the Tony Award. While at camp, she encouraged Charlotte and Portia to audition for Rachel Crothers's new musical. Crothers was also a director; her play *39 East* had garnered success. She was looking for musical numbers for her new play, a spinoff musical titled *Spring Magic*. The women spent months with no pay creating costumes, sets and the dance routine for the squirrels that were to frolic in Central Park in the play. The play opened in October 1926 to poor reviews, but Charlotte and Portia's act, *Squirrels and Girls*, was a hit.

Crothers offered half payment for their work but said she would help get the act on vaudeville. *Squirrels and Girls* hit the vaudeville circuit in 1927 and at one time had four acts going at once. They toured across the United States for three years on the Keith and Orpheum circuits, with the occasional hiccup, such as one of the dancers contracting scarlet fever and the girls imbibing in alcohol for the first time before a Canadian performance. *Squirrels and Girls* is believed to be the first vaudeville act to travel coast to coast and up into Montreal, British Columbia and Victoria.[77]

When film with sound was released, vaudeville began to change. In 1928, two new Portia Mansfield companies—the Rainbow Revelry and the Color and Rhythm Company (later renamed the Lee Twins Company)—were touring the Orpheum and Loews circuits, respectively. Summer camp was often used as a testing ground for vaudeville acts, and the final performance of 1929 excited the natives of Steamboat. African dance with masks by instructor Alice Paine Paul was accompanied by "barbaric tunes with tom-toms, rattles and other devices."[78] The show, which featured African sky

Right: The Silver Spruce Theater continues to host performances each year. *Author's collection.*

Below: The popular vaudeville act *Squirrels and Girls* toured concurrently on four different circuits. *Photograph by Nasib; Perry-Mansfield Archives.*

maidens come to earth, included African American melodies and spirituals and was slated as one of the last vaudeville acts created for the Portia Mansfield Dancers.

In 1930, the ladies heard reports of their booker using a color wheel on the medieval cathedral dance and ordering the nuns' costumes to be slit to the waist! When another booker tried to convince the manager of the Portia Mansfield Dancers to give him $200 from each booking, Charlotte paid him a visit in person. She demanded her money. When he refused, she threatened to pull all four companies off tour. The booker realized she was serious, so Charlotte was paid in cash and given a kiss as a bonus.[79]

It was time, they decided, to close down their acts and move on.

CAMP DURING THE VAUDEVILLE YEARS

1927

The ladies made time during their hectic schedules to travel to Italy, Spain, the Riviera, Paris and Africa. Their travels influenced their dances. Upon their return to Denver, they directed the *Pageant of Colorado* for Denver Music Week. Later that year, the State of New York invited them to direct the dance portion for *Saratoga Springs' Pageant* celebrating the 150th anniversary of the battle there during the American Revolution. "The pageant will be held on the famous battlefield, with a thousand dancers on the stage which will be about one fourth of a mile square. This affair is to be one of the most magnificent and spectacular out-door performances ever presented anywhere. President Coolidge and other famous officials are expected to be there," reported the *Steamboat Pilot* on August 19, 1927.

At summer camp, Charlotte turned her attention to theater, where her true passions lay. She directed her first play, *Rich Man; Poor Man*, "to unusual success....The scenic effects, the costuming and the lighting required to carry out the dream story were magnificent, and titillating were the feats performed by the actors in the dream scene," reported the *Steamboat Pilot*.[80] As the vaudeville years wound down, Charlotte became more and more involved in theater, while the day-to-day operations of camp fell to Portia.

1928

The success of the Perry-Mansfield Dancers attracted some of the top modern dancers and renowned composer Louis Horst to camp. Horst composed for Martha Graham and the Denishawn Company. He started the journal *Dance Observer*. At camp, his morning periods included over one hundred campers from all departments. "As they lay in the grasses soaking up the early morning sun, Mr. Horst played compositions ranging from Haydn to Beethoven through to the ultra-modern. Each piece was followed by a criticism and discussion."[81] Edna McRae, "the Grand Dame of Chicago's Ballet Mistresses," led dance that year. The curriculum continued to evolve in order to offer instruction for professional dancers, physical directors and educational teachers of dance.[82] To help keep camp running, Ramayeo Yeomans, a student of the early days of camp, returned to serve as secretary to the ladies for the next ten years. Charlotte Perry began directing the drama department, which she headed for almost forty years.

Louis Horst and Martha Graham. *Perry-Mansfield Archives.*

1929

Integration of the arts with a healthy lifestyle not only made P-M unique among dance camps but also allowed it to expand the camp in directions other arts camps couldn't to in order to survive financially. In 1929, Recreative Camp for Women was announced. The camp was designed to bring out the beauty and grace of a woman's body and mind. "Women who attend the health camp will learn how to achieve a youthful silhouette, a clear complexion, be adjusted mentality and [experience] buoyant health."[83] Campers were given access to the schools of dance, drama and the arts, as well as horseback riding, tennis, golf, swimming, badminton, auto trips, campfires, picnics and entertainment. Sunbaths were encouraged. "The miraculous results of sunbaths have been tested by leading physicians and proved by our own camp experience. For this reason all schedules include daily sunbaths under the supervision of the camp nurse." Sunbaths were taken in the nude in a "private place screened by canvas."[84]

On October 24, 1929, the stock market crashed, and the Great Depression began.

1930

The New York headquarters were moved from 10 Mitchell Street to a farm in Upstate New York, which was dubbed Perry-Mansfield Club. The club was "a place where friends and family could gather for weekends or short vacations from Oct 1 to June 1. Visitors were welcome to ride horseback, study plastiques with Portia and feast on delicious cuisine."[85]

In New York, Portia studied equitation under Captain Vladimir S. Littauer, who opened Boots and Saddles Riding School in New York. He promoted the forward riding system, focusing on the rider's position on the horse, balance, control and instruction of the horse in order to promote the horse's natural agility, balance and well-being. The system was developed around the idea that riding should be cooperative between rider and horse instead of dominating, a style Portia incorporated into the equestrian program at camp.[86]

Days in New York were just as full as days in Steamboat. While Portia worked often, not returning home until 10:30 p.m., Charlotte spent her days teaching in Greenwich, riding her horse, cleaning up the house, studying and going to bed around 10:30. Their schedule included commutes to New

Club Camp for Adults invited wealthy families from across the country to experience wilderness camp for themselves. This camp helped fund the dance and theater programs. *Perry-Mansfield Archives.*

York City to teach, studying at the Chalif School of Dance, having lunch with friends, teaching in the afternoons and staying the night with Helen Smith. Charlotte detailed a day in her life in a letter she sent home to her mother in 1929:

> *I miss you Peachum,*
> *I cooked, and washed dishes and ironed and made beds and talked and showed movies and rode and yet 10 p.m. I feel as fresh as a daisy....I had strained* [my back] *in some way possibly driving the new car or doing a new corrective* [a movement Portia created] *called "Hip, hip away."*
>
> *Fri: 8:00 a.m. teach correctives to Mrs. Watson on Park Ave.*
> *8:45 get breakfast*
> *9:00–12:00 classes at Progresium Ed. Soc. School*
> *12–1:30 lunch*
> *1:30–5:30 classes again*
> *5:30–7:30 teach Helen's boys and girls*
> *8:00 dinner stay Helen's Hotel* [87]

Rustic living quarters offered campers and counselors a true wilderness experience. *Perry-Mansfield Archives.*

With their earnings, more buildings were added in Steamboat, including Tree Tent, Top Tent, Tentament, Skyline, South Stage and North Barn. Camp programs now included the dance and theater programs; Recreation Camp; Junior Camp, an offshoot of recreation camp geared toward young campers; Ranger Camp for Boys; and Health Camp "for those who are either too fat or too thin which prescribes special diet and special exercises and has special quarters, but gives the same opportunities to enjoy the featured advantages of the other camps," reported the *Steamboat Pilot*.

In dance, Martha Graham's violent tension and release technique, and Doris Humphrey's form of dance originating in the spine and moving outward to the extremities were taught side by side. Dancing costumes consisted of a short, belted sleeveless smock of crêpe de chine, sateen dancing trunks, brassieres, opera-length stockings or socks, two pairs of ballet slippers, one pair of canvas soft toe shoes, one hard toe of pink satin and rompers for acrobatics. Additional camp necessities included a mackinaw or heavy coat, a sweater, a flannel nightgown, a canteen for horseback trips, an extra blanket or steamer rug, white breeches or knickers, one pair of high-heeled slippers for Spanish technique, castanets and musical instruments. A few items were available from camp, such as dancing costumes with batik design for ten dollars, trunks for two dollars or a shaded scarf for five dollars.[88]

In 1930, Portia earned a master's degree from New York University in health education, which she would use as a background for developing unique stretches and exercises called correctives.

3

CORRECTIVES

1931

Portia launched her correctives in New York. At NYU, Portia studied joints and balance in the joints. While assisting Dr. Lawton, diagnostician and head of the Department of Health and Physical Education at Queens College, she learned the importance of good posture, which she felt would translate to dancers. Through Dr. Lawton, Portia was given letters of introduction to the heads of hospitals and orthopedic hospitals. At one institution, the doctor who took Portia around said, "It's so simple. You grow in the way you sit or stand or walk. That's going to be your posture. You can't help it unless you pull yourself out of that and not let yourself fall into those positions."[89] Portia asked herself what it would take to pull someone out of poor posture or, in other words, correct the position of one's body. Using a mirror, she played around with posture and movement and found positions that helped joints settle differently. The results were presented to physical education and dance teachers during a seminar in New York. Charlotte gave the opening talk:

> *Now what I want you to remember today is that these correctives we are going to show you are not to be thought of merely in connection with the poor unfortunates. Instead they are meant for you, correct and handsome as you are! All that you have to do is look about you at the people we have assembled here to realize that we consider correctives to be the concern of*

Portia's Correctives in action. *Perry-Mansfield Archives.*

the normal, the fit, and in fact the superior person.... We believe, in short, that they are for everyone who wants to become or to stay fit and to live as efficiently and comfortably and gracefully as possible.... The first number of this program will be a few of the class exercises which will help prevent and correct three common faults, mainly sway back, round shoulders, and protruding abdomen.[90]

Correctives in rhythmic and dance form were exercises done in dance formations and combinations set to music composed by Louis Horst. According to the *Steamboat Pilot*, the exercises quickly became "in demand throughout the public and private schools of New York City and surrounding areas and demonstrations were given throughout the east and used by one of the largest gymnastic schools in England."[91]

The exercises were so popular Portia brought them to camp. This had two benefits. One, silhouettes were taken of every camper at the beginning and end of each season. The camper then had to take responsibility for improving his or her posture over the course of camp by taking Portia's correctives each morning. Campers were encouraged to improve weight issues by exercising, implementing healthy sleep patterns, relaxing and taking sunbaths.[92]

The second benefit was that teachers from across the country came to P-M to learn correctives in order to teach them at their own institutions, which increased the camp's revenue.[93] Three booklets were released: *Sixty Exercises in Rhythmic Movement, Correctives in Dance Form* and *Perry-Mansfield Correctives in Rhythmic Design: Book Three: Gymnastica.*

As the fad of correctives took off across the country, regular women wondered how they could improve their figures. In response, Portia designed exercises to help the average woman slim down. Her exercises were written up in the *New York Sun* and said to help improve mood and attain balance "between the emotional, the physical and the mental."[94] Portia's correctives eventually made their way around the world.

A CENTER FOR MODERN DANCE

1931

In 1931, Virginia Tanner showed up at P-M. When she arrived, she insisted on a meeting with the ladies. She said she had no money but would work in exchange for lessons. The ladies initially said they had no work, but when she asked again, they allowed her to stay the night. In the morning, she was put to work in the kitchen and given permission to take a dance class. She worked tirelessly that year and was invited back the following year. Seeing her dedication, Charlotte lessened Tanner's workload so she could focus more on dance.[95]

Virginia Tanner. *Perry-Mansfield Archives.*

When Tanner returned to her home in Utah, she taught. She directed the dance department of the McCune School of Music and Art in Salt Lake City in the 1940s before organizing the Children's Dance Theatre Program (CDT) in 1949, which became permanently affiliated with the University of Utah. In 1953, the children danced at the Jacob's Pillow Dance Theatre in Massachusetts, the American Dance Festival in Connecticut and New York University's summer camp in Upstate New York.[96] Her students made the cover of *LIFE* magazine when they danced on the steps of the Capitol in Washington, D.C.

1932

New campers were initiated into P-M's world with a progressive dinner their first night:

> *The dinner began with hors d'ouvres in the professional house, soup at the clan house, chop suey from the bowl of the Chinese chef at the club camp, dessert in the theater and coffee served in the junior house. In the theater, long tables lighted by many candles ran thru the theater and onto the stage where the background gave an effect of a medieval banquet. The great log fire and tall candles threw long shadows on the wall. The festivity of the evening was a huge bonfire and marshmallow roast at the highest point on the senior hill.*
>
> *The program given throughout the dinner was the reading of the supposed diary of the first camper who ever came to P.M.C. This camper went thru all the trials and tribulations of any camper of any year—the slight touch of homesickness, the misplacing of articles, the loss of laundry, and so on. This skit was written by Verner Haldene, dramatic instructor, and was most successfully carried out by Martha Castles....Miss Castles, dressed in an ancient green velvet riding habit that once belonged to the wardrobe of Charlotte Perry herself, acted as the first camper, Ivy Tassel, who read excerpts from her diary during each course. When the campers were eating at the club camp they were astounded by the sudden arrival of a very dilapidated buggy drawn by an equally downcast white horse. In the driver's seat was Marjorie Perry accompanied by Helen Howbert and Mrs. Edith Smith. They went thru the joys and sorrows of the old days when driving a singular rig to and from town after butter, eggs, groceries, coal, wood and campers was an absolute necessity.[97]*

Across the country, Bennington College in Vermont launched a new summer dance program. The school created competition for P-M, as it was easier to access for many of their East Coast students and boasted a staff of the top modern dancers of the day. Fortunately, the arrival of Doris Humphrey in 1932 secured P-M's place as a hub for instruction in modern dance. Humphrey created the technique of fall and recovery, which Portia filmed on the hills of camp. That summer Humphrey performed *Water Study*, one of the first unaccompanied dances ever created, and *Parade*, a comment on how people behave unobserved and unconsciously while watching a passing parade.[98]

1933

Hanya Holm, one of the pioneers of modern dance, taught at P-M in the summer of 1933. She studied under Mary Wigman in Germany and later opened Wigman Dance Studio in New York. During World War II, in response to American prejudices against Germans, the studio was named the Hanya Holm School of Dance. She later choreographed dances for Broadway's *Kiss Me Kate*, *My Fair Lady* and *Camelot*. Holm believed dancers should *feel* movement instead of watching movement in mirrors.

Campers packed for a three-day camping trip head into the rugged outdoors. *Perry-Mansfield Archives.*

Hanya Holm. *Courtesy of Marianne Elser; Perry-Mansfield Archives.*

From 1930 to 1950, Margaret B. Chase conducted mountain pack trips and served as the photographer for the Perry-Mansfield Theater School. Chase, née Blackford, was later trained as a member of the Apollo Mission Planning Task Force for the Apollo moon landing project. Expeditions that year included a trip to Vernal, Utah, for the Sun Dance Festival of the Ute Indians and an expedition to the Sand Wash Basin to watch the wild horse round-up. After the season ended, campers were invited to stay on for an excursion to the Indian pueblos near Taos and then on to Santa Fe, New Mexico, for the fall festivals of the Navajo and Hopi Indians.[99]

1934

Enrollment at camp dropped to eighty students, but at the same time, the caliber of instructors was continuing to increase. Tina Flade, also connected with the Wigman School of Dance, taught that summer. Flade

Tina Flade (*second from left*). *Perry-Mansfield Archives.*

had polio as a child yet climbed to the top of Hahns Peak, an elevation of over ten thousand feet, without breathing heavily. Fritzie Moore, a staple at camp for many years, directed the tap department, while Paul Boepple, the director of the Dalcroze Institute, taught the Dalcroze method to all of camp and, by Charlotte's account, was one of the most exciting teachers they had. Portia headed dance composition and choreography.[100] Despite the decrease in campers, two new buildings—Two Tent and Music Room—were constructed.

That winter, Portia served as director of the dance department of the Peabody Conservatory of Music in Baltimore, Maryland, while Charlotte directed drama. Charlotte also taught drama at the Bureau of Educational Experiments in New York and at the Rosemary Elementary School in Greenwich, Connecticut.

1935

At camp, 1935 was an electric year. Portia was named to the Who's Who of Women in America. The combination of instructors that summer was perhaps the pinnacle of modern dance at P-M. José Limón, Agnes de Mille and Louise Kloepper taught, while Harriette Ann Gray attended her first summer as a student. When Limón showed an interest in theater, Charlotte offered him the part of a duke in a Florentine medieval tragedy. His role was to open a door, walk down six steps and tell everyone to join him during the plague. Before the show began on opening night, the crew, aware of his excitable nature, warned him, "This is only a set, so be gentle with the door."

"The first thing he did was to take hold of the doorframe and lift it so hard that he pulled it from the hinges and held it in his hand. The stagehands whispered, 'Put the door down! Just put the door down!' Charlotte and the other actors were almost wild. So he put the door down, came down the steps and fell flat on his face!"[101]

His dance performances were much more widely regarded and were considered "one of the outstanding features of the first production of camp that summer. His pupils danced a four-episode number without music, interpreting the Depression and mob spirit in following professed leaders only to be disappointed. The interpretation was given entirely through body movements, facial expressions and rhythm."[102]

One day, when Limón was bored, Charlotte suggested he paint the cabinets and fireplace in Cabeen. Limón had once aspired to be a visual artist. Both Charlotte and Portia were stunned when they came home to find he had used the cabinets and fireplace as a canvas for his art. Years later, the ladies took the cabinets off their hinges and transported them to their home in Carmel. The art he painted around the fireplace at Cabeen remains to this day.

Agnes de Mille also made an impression that summer. De Mille has been credited as being one of the first choreographers to give dance a prominent role in film. Until that time, dance was used as filler in both stage and film productions and was not integral to the storyline. De Mille changed that with her choreography for *Oklahoma!*, *Carousel*, *Brigadoon*, *Gentlemen Prefer Blondes*, *Rodeo* and many other Broadway productions. That summer, de Mille asked Portia if she would take her to see a good old-fashioned hoedown. She was working on a solo dance that she had begun in New York, in which she'd been dressed in a sunbonnet and pioneer dress. Charlotte and Portia took her up to the Elkhead Rock School House out past Hayden for a big square dance.

When they arrived, the women were seated on one side and the men lined the other. No one had ventured out to the dance floor yet. The ancient and bearded fiddlers played a lively tune. Charlotte exclaimed that this was the tune Aggie needed for her solo dance. She goaded, "These people have

Left: Agnes de Mille. *Perry-Mansfield Archives.*

Right: José Limón. *Perry-Mansfield Archives.*

never seen your kind of dance. I dare you to get up and do it and see what the result is."[103] Fearless, Aggie jumped into the center of the dance floor and began her solo dance.

> *Conversation halted. The cowboys on the sidelines couldn't believe it. They sat up and got so excited! "That's it, girlie!" they called. "You get 'im! Go to it!" They kept at it through the whole thing. Toward the end they began to whisper together, and no one knew what was going on. Just as it ended, they formed a line with Aggie at the end and they "cracked the whip" out the big door of the schoolhouse, sailing her out over the sagebrush. She landed flat down. When she got up, she said, "That's what I call success!"*[104]

Enchanted with de Mille, a young camper, Richard Pleasant, approached her and told her he was going to hire her to dance for him one day. Pleasant was a nephew of Ferry Carpenter's but came from Maybell, a town of twenty-five people. He had no talent for dance but recognized it in others. Many years later, he started American Ballet Theatre with Lucia Chase. His first season, he kept his promise and hired de Mille, who opened the 1940 season with *Black Ritual*. This was the first time an all–African American cast had been used in a major dance company.

As a student, Harriette Ann Gray could not have picked a better year to begin camp. She immediately became a darling of Portia's and a protégé of José Limón. She studied drama with Charlotte. Through the combination of these studies, her dancing came to embody the expressive P-M dance-drama technique. Limón introduced Gray to Charles Weidman and Doris Humphrey, and she became the principal dancer for the Humphrey-Weidman Dance Company. Her technique was so unparalleled that she was used as a technical barometer for their choreography. It is said that if Gray could not perform a move then it wasn't shown to the rest of the dancers.

The following year, Gray returned to instruct in dance. She taught until 1946, when she took over the dance department until 1979. During her career, she founded two dance companies and two studios in New York City. In Hollywood, in the 1940s, she trained celebrities Rita Hayworth, Ann Miller and Tony Curtis. She was hired as a dancer-choreographer for Columbia, United Artists and Warner Brothers motion picture studios and performed in *The Joison Story* and *Down to Earth*. She went on to head Stephens College's Dance Department. Gray let her students know, "There are only two kinds of dancing, good and bad."[105] She believed that to achieve dance that was honest and inspired, a dancer must first be sensitive and aware.[106] Gray defined the dance department at P-M for many years.

1936

When Charlotte wanted to improve her acting, Louis Horst recommended she take classes with Madame Maria Ouspenskaya of the Moscow Art Theatre at her School of Dramatic Art in New York. Her classes attracted up-and-coming actors as well as those already established in their fields.

> *When Charlotte knocked on Madame's door and asked if she could observe the class, Madame insisted, "No. You haf to be in a class."*
> *Charlotte said, "But all these people are so much younger."*
> *"I vil be tactful," the teacher replied.*
> *The first thing she did, with a twinkle in her eye, was to cast Charlotte, who at the time was forty-seven years old, as a bride of sixteen in* The Daughter of Jorio *by D'Annunzio.*[107]

Some women found the camping trips exhausting. *Perry-Mansfield Archives.*

The techniques she learned were brought back to camp, especially the notion of first acting as an animal to later portray animal characteristics in people.

In the spring of 1936, Portia trained one thousand dancers for a pageant, *The History of Costume*, presented at the stadium of Brown University in Providence, Rhode Island, to celebrate the Rhode Island tercentenary. She was also elected the first female president of the American Camping Association.

Summer brought pack trips, big game hunting, sage chicken hunting, wild horse runs and fishing trips to the timberline lakes. Additional trips were offered to observe Indian ceremonial dances and visit Zion, Bryce and Mesa Verde National Parks.

Eleanor King, formerly a member of the Humphrey-Weidman Dance Group, brought the flavor of the Orient to camp after studying kabuki in Japan. Barney Brown of the Pasadena Community Playhouse served as technical and dramatic director, instructor of stage production, lighting and make-up. Brown worked with Charlotte for many years.

In order to bridge the gap between local ranching families and young artists, students could pay extra to spend time on a ranch. The girls were

Above: Eleanor King. *Perry-Mansfield Archives.*

Opposite, top: Campers could pay extra money to spend time at local ranches, where they would be invited to help feed animals and pitch in with daily chores. *Perry-Mansfield Archives.*

Opposite, bottom: Square dancing parties helped integrate Perry-Mansfield into the Steamboat Springs community. *Perry-Mansfield Archives.*

put to work milking cows and feeding lambs, calves and chickens. Those who knew how were welcome to ride horseback on cow round-ups or shoot pistols at a target. Excursions were offered from the ranches, including hiking Hahn's Peak or panning for gold. A few girls even found rubies.[108] In addition to payment, boys from the Wheeler and Carpenter ranches were often invited to P-M for square dances. As another means of ingratiating themselves with the community, P-M held a Strawberry Park Fiesta and Barbeque in which neighbors in the Strawberry Park area were invited to watch a parade, sing songs, dance and eat.

1937

By 1937, Portia and Charlotte were teaching in seven different schools in New York, including the Rosemary Upper and Junior Schools, the Bedford Rippowam Country-Day School, the Little Red School House, the Bureau for Educational Experiments, the Vocational Service for Juniors and the PTA of Mamaroneck Junior High School.[109] In 1938, Portia added the Dwight School in Englewood and the Greenwich Country Day School in Bedford, New York, to her winter teaching schedule.

Summer at P-M brought camper Joey Luckie Rigsby, who came to study violin and viola under Alix Young Marichess. Her solo concert was well remembered by Steamboat residents, and Rigsby became a lifelong supporter of Perry-Mansfield, as did many other students whose lives were changed by their experiences in the wilderness of Steamboat Springs.

5

BARNSTORMING

1939

By 1939, camp had been in session for twenty-five consecutive years. New units, Top Notch and Three Trees, were built for college students. This was also the year barnstorming began. From 1939 through the early 1940s, Charlotte organized tours of theater and dance, somewhat like their vaudeville days, but instead of playing at the Palace or Grauman's, Charlotte created her own circuit of shows traveling from college campuses and barns to schoolhouses, ranches and theaters throughout Colorado and Wyoming. They visited the University of Wyoming in Laramie, gold miners in Hahns Peak and ranchers across the West. Everyone looked forward to the visits. The first performance given, *What So Proudly We Hail*, was an original work written by Charlotte Perry. Barney Brown staged the play, with dances arranged by Charles Weidman, Harriette Ann Gray, Portia and Fritzie Moore. Drusa Wilker of Vassar College composed and arranged the music, Louis Webber was in charge of costumes and Gray, Brown and Lowell Whiteman were part of the cast.

Ranchers, cowboys and their families traveled from nearly one hundred miles away to see their first show. The subject matter, the first 150 years of American colonists' hopes and fears, did not resonate, and they received only polite acknowledgement. The only positive response they received was from a couple of World War I veterans, including an imposing rancher who "slapped his thigh with his ten-gallon hat and exclaimed, 'If we'd a-knowed

Israeli Suite. *Perry-Mansfield Archives.*

this was what you was goin' to put on we'd a-had the whole American Legion up here.'"[110] However, as soon as the dancing and pantomime began, the audience loosened up. Charles Weidman's Cowboy Dance elicited the most enthusiastic response of the nights, with whoops and hollering.

> *The barnstorming tour finished at Andy Anderson's famous A Bar A Ranch near Encampment in Wyoming. They were surrounded by mountains that ended in the rolling twenty-thousand-acre ranch where cattle grazed. For the first time, the actors and dancers would be performing for "sophisticates." By this time, the crew was ready for anything, including costume changes in the harness room and oat bin, a mezzanine of new-mown hay and the smells and sounds of cows and horses below. Fortunately, the audience was immediately engaged with the play, and their enthusiasm only grew as the performance went on.*[111]

The following year, Perry's play *And a Time to Dance* was taken on tour. The title of the play was taken from the scriptural quote "A time to be born and a time to die. A time to mourn and a time to dance." The play tells the story of the people who made America during the 1870s, '80s, '90s, the first world war, the boom days, the Depression and the present day through the dances of the day that included square dances, quadrille, ballet, tap, Castle walk, Maxxie, bunny hug, lynch town, beer barrel polka and jitterbug. "The action opens in a 1940 cabaret where groups listened to the latest war news. Amazed, they stopped short to hear, even in the midst of a dance. Then with placid indifference the dance was resumed."[112] The play exposed the country's struggles and triumphs and the song and dance that connected past to present and human beings from all walks of life.

Barnstorming allowed students to act alongside their instructors, experience the West and all its varying cultures and return to a simpler way of life where beds might be on a pile of straw or luxurious guest cottages at a ranch, where instinct and improvising became a way of life for a short time. Barnstorming ended in the 1940s, when World War II prevented travel.

6
THE WAR YEARS

1940

In 1940, Ranch Camp opened for transient guests affected by the war. Mrs. Elliot Ritchie of Boston served as hostess to guests coming for an overnight or weekly stay.[113] An infirmary and Cliff Palace were built.

Throughout the years, Portia produced films of dance on campus and rented them for educational purposes. *The Ballad of the Little Square*, suggested by the poem of Federico García Lorca, a seven-minute slow-motion film of impressions of dancer Harriette Ann Gray, was purchased by the U.S. Information Service to be shown throughout Europe. *Dance Demonstration*, another of Portia's films, was translated for use in India.[114] In the United States, her films traveled the country—from the Dance Symposium of the Southwest in San Diego, California, to schools and colleges on the East Coast.[115]

Guest instructors for the season included Mildred Zook of Chicago for square dancing and Elizabeth Waters for modern dance. Valerie Bettis attended as a student. She returned later to teach. Bettis was the first modern dancer to choreograph for a major ballet company with *Virginia Sampler* in 1947 for the Ballet Russe de Monte Carlo. She worked for Hollywood and Broadway and brought back to dance a concept of "total theater," the combined use of singing, dancing and acting in such ballets as *As I Lay Dying* and *A Streetcar Named Desire*.

The theater workshop premiered *Run, Peddler, Run*, an original play by Charlotte Perry. The play takes place during the "bound" period, when young girls had to earn their passage from Europe to America and would be bound for seven years with the same person who brought them across. The backdrop of the play was the witch hunts and the difficulties women of that era faced. Some became peddlers traveling from one place to the next. The play was later produced by Junior Programs Inc. of New York and toured during 1939 and 1940, with Barney Brown playing the lead. In all, the play was given a seventeen-run tour across the country.

1941

With the success of Charlotte's plays, she began publishing articles on the benefits of acting. She believed a child's personality could be changed through different exercises, such as giving an introverted child an extroverted role. Her pantomime exercises enabled students to use the body as an instrument of expression. The drama program included analysis of plays for production, comedies, makeup, designing, construction, painting and scenery, lighting and costume design—including painting and dyeing costumes—as well as the psychology of the effects in line and color of costumes.[116] By learning each of the skills that go into creating the complete theatrical experience, students

gained a greater appreciation not only for acting but also for how acting becomes an illusion. To bring out the best performances in her students, Charlotte could often be heard saying, "I don't believe you!"

1942

When the United States entered World War II, P-M reinvented its summer program to support the war effort. On top of the dance and drama courses, the camp offered the following:

Charlotte Perry teaching theater to her students. *Perry-Mansfield Archives.*

War Preparation Leadership Course

- American Red Cross courses in first aid and nutrition
- Field duty: camp, town, ranch and mining groups
- Gardening, with and without irrigation
- Commissary and canteen work

Work in Conservation

- Clearing barbed wire from fields, draining wet pastures
- Clearing and improving roads, trails and fords
- Repairing washouts, irrigation ditches and fences
- Pruning and watering young trees
- Exterminating rodents

Winter Evacuation Center

Preparation of Camps for Possible Winter Use and Protection Against Fire in Our National Forests

- Burying pipelines, banking foundations
- Reinforcing and insulating cabin walls
- Digging trenches and vegetable cellars
- Installing stoves, insulating tank[117]

Girls were put to work picking wild raspberries for camp meals. Students packed their own horses for outings and learned to tie a diamond hitch. They planted potatoes and fixed barbed-wire fences. Closing an irrigation ditch and learning to chop wood "how Charlotte *thinks* it should be done," Portia joked, were ways in which women could train to take over the farming responsibilities left by men gone to war.

The equestrian program taught campers how to round up cattle, wrangle horses, snake logs and blaze and clear trails. The local blacksmith taught the girls to shoe a horse as well as how to saddle, harness and drive a team. A horse-drawn wagon was built by campers and the canvas cover painted in order to take trips into town—or to use in the event of an evacuation. Gymkhana, rodeos and horse shows continued to take place, with proceeds

During World War II, covered wagons were once again used to transport campers. *Perry-Mansfield Archives.*

going to the Red Cross. Each staff member pledged two hours of instruction to the war program. Campers were encouraged to do the same. A junior unit of the American Women's Voluntary Services (AWVS) was formed.

Julie Harris, a student at P-M for the first time, arrived to study dance. Charlotte immediately recognized her talent for acting and encouraged her to pursue the stage. At camp, she worked in the kitchen to pay off her scholarship. In 1943, her second year, she walked two miles to town and two miles back (in order to conserve gasoline and tires) to teach drama to local children. At P-M, she played the lead in *The Swan* opposite Merce Cunningham and starred in *Four Walls* with Merce Cunningham, Leora Dana and Virginia Tanner with décor by Arch Lauterer and music by John Cage. She also starred in *Vain Shadow* with Valerie Bettis and Leora Dana. Soon after leaving Perry-Mansfield, she obtained special permission to enter the Yale University Drama School as their youngest student. Harris went on to win five Tony Awards for her work on Broadway.

"Working with Charlotte was the first time someone looked at me with love and affection and believed in me. It was like the sunshine pouring on flowers, you just opened up with all that intensity of Kingo's light on you....I owe Miss Perry a great deal. It was largely through her encouragement that

In the equestrian program, students learned how to dance on horseback. *Perry-Mansfield Archives.*

I decided to continue in the theater," said Harris when interviewed for the film *A Divine Madness*, by Len Aitken.[118]

Charlotte chose the play *Letters to Lucerne*—a story about how war problems affect students in a boarding school in neutral Switzerland—for that year's production. The cast featured Sage Fuller and Leora Dana. For the Fourth of July parade, Portia taught the equestrian students how to dance on horseback, fulfilling her childhood dream. The only down note at camp that summer was Clan House catching on fire late one night. As counselors and campers passed buckets of water down the line to put out the fire, Portia filmed the happenings. Finally, the U.S. Forest Service extinguished the fire. Early the next morning, the cooks put together a pancake breakfast. At that time, the "disheveled pair of directors met in the doorway of the kitchen. Portia, from out of nowhere, handed Charlotte a single, bright flower, slightly dilapidated. The firemen broke out in applause."[119]

1943

No men were available to open camp, so the staff pitched in. They repaired roofs, mended fences, planted gardens, opened the cabins and cleared trails so that all was ready when the campers came. Campers, for their part, were warned to pack lightly and leave wardrobe trunks home as they would have to transport their own luggage.

Girls were expected to take the place of men through mowing fields and stacking hay. "Knowing that you have helped provide food for a herd of cattle for the next nine months is compensation for the times on the stack when you thought you'd scream if they brought up another load!"[120] Fortunately, all hard work at camp was rewarded. To release tension and reclaim a measure of good old-fashioned fun, a square dance was put on each week with Steamboat's famous Wheeler family band playing.

1944

In August 1944, Merce Cunningham, who danced with the Martha Graham Dance Company before founding the Merce Cunningham Dance Company, staged *Four Walls*. Monies from the play were donated to the National War Fund, a fund designed to support entertainment for service men and women throughout the world. *Four Walls* marked the first large-scale collaboration between Merce Cunningham and composer John Cage. The story dealt with a dysfunctional American family as the members descended into madness.[121] The play was filmed by Portia.

Camper Frank Glass studied with Cunningham that year. Glass was the first black dancer at Perry-Mansfield. Up until then, the camp had never had a black student, and Portia and Charlotte weren't sure who to house him with to ensure a kind and safe environment, as racism still existed throughout the country. Fortunately, one of the campers, Ronnie Kaplan, who was also out to take dance, came to the ladies and asked to be his roommate. Glass was chosen for Harriette Ann Gray's dance company. Glass was a talented dancer and an aspiring writer. He hoped that some editor would accept and publish one of his stories. While he didn't encounter racism at Perry-Mansfield, he did in New York City, where he couldn't get a job dancing, so he ran an elevator. He later committed suicide.

During the war years, horses became critical for camp to continue running smoothly. They were once again used for transportation in order to save on fuel and tires. Classes in care for horses and practical uses of harnessing them drew in campers. Horses became a beautiful necessity.

7
EQUESTRIAN PROGRAM

The riding program at Perry-Mansfield was a primary component of the camp experience from the beginning. When Marjorie Perry first headed the program, she considered a "good rider" someone who could stay in the saddle even when stung by a bee. She taught western riding, a form of riding that used a saddle with a horn, best suited for travel over uneven ground, rounding up cattle and riding over rocky mountains.

After the vaudeville years, Portia wanted to increase the visibility of the equestrian program. At the Boulder Brook Club in New York where she rode, she met Frank Carroll, a nationally recognized instructor in English riding and horse jumping. She recruited him to teach. Carroll's presence helped build P-M's reputation as a destination for equestrian instruction.[122] Through Carroll, Perry-Mansfield was entered into the horse show at Madison Square Garden, the first camp ever to enter a team. The riders took second place during their second year and won ribbons both years.

In 1944, Elizabeth Shannon, who had originally come to camp as a dancer but fell in love with horses, took over the equestrian program, and she remained head of the riding department until 1979. Her daily uniform consisted of an ironed long-sleeved snap-front shirt, western slacks, conservative belt, boots and western hat and gloves (when she was riding). For harsher weather, she wore a long oilskin jacket.

In the early years of camp, riders wore wide jodhpurs, white button-down shirts and flowing scarves, but under Shannon's tutelage, they soon adapted themselves to a western outfit of blue Levis, a button-down shirt, a leather

The Perry-Mansfield equestrian program gained notoriety under the tutelage of Frank Carroll. *Perry-Mansfield Archives.*

belt, scuffed boots and a black cowboy hat from the local store F.M. Light & Sons. Shannon was both loved and feared by campers. The care and well-being of the horses was always a top priority. Saddle blankets had to be smooth, cinches not too tight. Riding students were referred to as "barn rats." Her favorites—girls who worked hard and were polite and respectful and didn't smoke—were invited to go to square dances with her and movie nights in Cabeen.

In order to set the equestrian program above other programs, Shannon, with Portia's help, instituted the first English Riding Rating Center in the West at P-M. Ratings followed a national standard and allowed those with certificates to teach. Judges from New York came out to give a clinic before the Rating Center Judging. As part of their outreach to the Steamboat community, P-M offered courses to Routt County residents for a nominal fee.[123]

In 1964, Shannon and Portia inaugurated the first Western Riding Rating Center in America under the auspices of the National Education Association (NEA). In 1970, the NEA published Shannon's book, *Manual for Teaching Western Riding*, thus finally giving western-style riding the respectability it deserved. She later founded the Northwestern Colorado Horse Show, which brought hundreds of people from across the country to Steamboat, where they could learn about the programs taking place at P-M. In 1977, Shannon received an NEA Horsemanship Award for her outstanding contribution to horsemanship in America and was later inducted into the Arizona Women's Hall of Fame.

For many years, there was a huge divide in attitudes toward English and western riding styles. Flat, or eastern, saddles were mocked as "postage stamps" and considered impractical by western riders. Eastern riders regarded western saddles—which you could "hang onto"—as pedestrian and felt that anyone could ride that way. P-M felt that

Instead of setting up standards for riding in different geographical areas (such as Western riding, Tennessee Walking Horses, etc., or different types of riding, hunting, polo, saddles), we should explore the possibility of one set of simple standards which would serve schools, colleges and camps. Was there not a basis on which all good riding rests?

We came to the conclusion that Basic Riding consists of:

Position or how to sit on the horse.
How to control the horse
How to school the horse.

We are not out to discourage specialties, such as hunting, showing…quite the contrary. All specialties which belong to the horseman will benefit from such knowledge.[124]

Shannon brought together ranchers, teachers and young riders and found the key element of good horsemanship was a forward position that gives the horse and rider a more balanced, controlled ride. Portia and Shannon went on to create several films on horsemanship, flat saddle basic riding and stock-saddle basic riding, including *Horsemanship Goes Forward*.[125]

Tuition at camp included two lessons and a trail ride each week. Extra lessons could be paid for or earned by helping take care of the ring, tack room or shoveling manure. As riders progressed, they earned bandanas for each level of training. Yellow ribbons were for beginners. Red bandanas showed you understood the first levels of horsemanship. Blue bandanas included a broader understanding of horses and diseases that can affect horses, pack trip etiquette and tack, as well as basic medicinal care for horses that have been injured. Purple bandana wearers had knowledge of breeds, shoeing and polo hunting. Bareback riding instruction was also offered.

For fun, gymkhanas—informal horse shows with games on horseback—were held. Riders played musical chairs on horseback, had to put on pajamas while riding and ate doughnuts off a string. Later, barrel races and slalom courses were added to the program. Overnight trips were offered in the 1930s and '40s for an extra seventy-five dollars per camper. The trips commenced no matter the weather. In Colorado, storms blow in quickly, and more than

Campers learned all aspects of taking care of their horses. *Perry-Mansfield Archives.*

once, riders had to tie their horses to trees and lie flat on the ground as lightning got closer. After dark, ghost stories were told around the campfires, and songs were sung. Tales of mountain lion hunts, grizzly bears and coyotes made it back to camp, prompting a young girl with pigtails to call out to an outfit leaving, "Bring me a mountain lion."[126]

While Shannon was very controlled in how she operated the equestrian program, other instructors embodied a wilder spirit of riding more reminiscent of Marjorie Perry's days. In 1957, Katee Pfeister came to P-M—initially to study with horsewoman Marianne MacRae. She returned to teach. "Katee's dad was part Cherokee, which showed itself through her dark hair, eyes and skin. The darkness contrasted with the silver bracelets she wore up to her elbows, earrings and necklaces. She flashed like lightning. She wore tight jeans and silver belt buckles —all prizes she had won in the rodeo. Her look was finished with a cowboy hat and boots. She relayed tales of her days on the rodeo circuit to campers and taught the girls the Code of the Cowgirl:

> 1. *Make sure your horse and tack are immaculate…then you get to take a shower.*
> 2. *Don't get shoved into corners in the show ring. Use your spurs on the leg of the culprit of "dirty horsemanship" so that person doesn't try to ever push you and your steed around again.*
> 3. *Shoveling manure when you are young teaches you what horse shit is, so you'll be able to recognize it when it pours from the mouths of politicians and other dubious characters.*[127]

"Katee's trail rides early in the mornings attracted her most loyal followers. Before Shannon woke up, as they brought in the horses from pasture they would gallop through the fields, jump ditches and hoot and holler! Her riding style relied on loose reins, legs and balance. Watching her ride her horse Skedaddle in complex reining patterns without a bridle, using only leg aids and balance was amazing,"[128] remembered camper Martine Richards Minnis.

At its peak, Perry-Mansfield housed approximately seventy-five horses, and the equestrian program rivaled the dance and theater programs in attendance. For dance students, riding horses helped those less graceful find balance and confidence, which easily translated back to the arts. By the 1970s, pack trips were phasing out, as there were too many fences, too many people and too many Jeeps riding up roads that used to be deserted.

In 2016, approximately fifteen horses resided at camp, with about half staying through the fall for after-school lessons. Two week-long equestrian camps are offered during the summers for ages ten to fourteen and two mini-equestrian camps of half days for children six to nine. Equestrian instruction is an elective available to dance and drama students, and more than half usually sign up. The program teaches horse care, horsemanship, basic dressage, jumping and trail/cross country riding. Western riding is offered, but it is limited. One trail ride is offered for each group of students, and non-mounted horse experiences are available for the Art Explorers and Art Fusion students.

Naomi Barker, head of the equestrian program, fell in love with camp in 2005 when she was a part-time instructor. In 2011, she took over as department head. "Having horses at camp lets students experience the history and culture of Steamboat Springs," said Barker. "The equestrian program is beneficial to dance and theater students because it combines strength, balance, flexibility, movement, coordination and cooperation. The experience with horses teaches students a lot about themselves and improves confidence."[129] Under P-M's new executive director, Nancy Engelken, the hopes are that even more students will find the balance horseback riding can bring to a hectic schedule.

8
POST WORLD WAR II

1945

After the war ended, Perry-Mansfield experienced its greatest attendance in history. In July, 160 students were set to arrive. Ranch camp for adults was kept open two weeks past the close of camp in order to replenish decreased revenues from the war years. Una Hanbury offered a course in sculpture, continuing the tradition of the arts from the earliest days of camp. Hanbury sculptures are housed in museums around the world. Given the caliber of work being produced at P-M in the summers, the University of Wyoming and New York University allowed graduate credits to be earned in certain classes.

1946

A young student, Frances Sternhagen, audited one of Charlotte's theater classes and flopped her first tryout. She then took advanced classes in dance with Harriette Ann Gray, where Gray referred to her as Poppins for her role in *Mary Poppins*. Gray could be heard calling impatiently, "Poppins! Faster!" "Poppins! Look UP!"[130] While she flopped her first tryout, Sternhagen didn't give up on acting. Her career went on to include roles on Broadway's *Driving Miss Daisy*, *The Good Doctor*, *Equus* and *On Golden Pond*. She was nominated for five Tony Awards.

Winter snows rest softly on your tents
Old trails are new white fields
That wait the mark of rabbits' feet
No smoke curls up against the hard
Bright sky, But all
The long sweet shadows
Of the aspens lie across the road that runs
From lodge to gate and out to fields again.

Left: A reunion invitation. The directors of Perry-Mansfield stayed in touch with campers throughout the year to keep camp fresh in their memories. *Perry-Mansfield Archives.*

Below: Portia Mansfield loved nothing more than to photograph dancers in nature. Her photography and, later, her films preserved an era of dances. *Perry-Mansfield Archives.*

As Portia closed up camp that year, she wrote in the winter *Pine Bark*, a newsletter that was sent to campers to keep P-M in their minds throughout the year, "Best of all is the 'amethyst glow' at sunset on old Storm its sides covered with golden aspens and its top covered with fresh snow. It seems to ask, 'Sister, why leave this country to go to a city?'"

1947

That winter, Charlotte began teaching and directing at the Theater Department of Hunter College. After her first week of teaching, she wrote home to her mother, "No lives lost and few spirits broken."[131] Her students had a different take on her. "Kingo was very businesslike until she talked about children's theater then she became a child herself. She was the most inspirational, imaginative, magical teacher I've ever had," said Rusty DeLucia, a former student of Charlotte's. "She could bring things out of people that you could never expect and she could look you right in the eye and tell you 'I don't believe you.' and you would take it because she was so passionate." DeLucia met Charlotte at Hunter College, when she was in fourth grade. By the time she was thirteen, she was invited to P-M for the summer. At fifteen, Charlotte had her teaching children's theater at P-M (even though she wasn't paid that year). Today, DeLucia continues to teach at P-M and carries on Charlotte's principles. Other students who showed talent in acting, including Ingrid Wekerle, were also invited to P-M's summer sessions to continue their studies.

When camp opened for the summer, approximately 150 campers arrived from across the United States, England, South America and the Canal Zone. The old coal stoves in the kitchens were finally replaced by oil burners, making the cooks' jobs easier and the food even tastier.[132] Instructors that year included Peggy Lawler, Iris Mabry and Nina Youskevitch, solo ballerina at the Metropolitan Opera House. Valerie Bettis and her husband, Bernardo Segall, returned for their third season teaching.

Charlotte launched another original play that season, *When Satan Hops Out*, with music by Harry John Brown, choreography by Harriette Ann Gray and set design by Arch Lauterer. The play premiered in Steamboat before playing at the historic Wheeler Opera House in Aspen.[133] *When Satan Hops Out*, based on a local story, takes place in Routt County, where a woman searching for her husband in a blizzard comes upon a remote rancher's

Ingrid Wekerle (*sitting left*) and Fred Jackson (*standing right*). *Perry-Mansfield Archives.*

cabin. The rancher finds the husband dead but must live with the woman for several months until spring arrives, when the husband's body can be buried and the rancher and the woman can safely travel to town. Both the devil and angels have starring roles to show conflict with the rancher about the temptation he feels being alone with this beautiful woman. In the play, angels were dressed in white costumes suggesting western clothes while the men wore wire halos designed to look like western hats. The women's halos were designed to suggest bonnets. God was dressed in gold and played a guitar.[134] The play was optioned to go on Broadway for two years, with Gene Kelly playing the lead. Unfortunately, the option was never fulfilled. However, based on the strength of her play, Charlotte became the first alumna of Smith College to be awarded first prize in its playwriting contest for most outstanding play written in the past year.

1948

Buses transported campers to Steamboat from Denver for the first time. The camp program stressed the integration of dance and drama. Students of each discipline were required to spend a portion of each day studying the alternate disciplines in order to create a well-rounded understanding of the arts and increase collaboration between disciplines.

Lucile Bogue was one of the campers who fully embraced the necessity of cultural and artistic integration in education. She later went on to found the Yampa Valley College (now Colorado Mountain College) in 1962 with Charlotte and Portia's support. Her memories of camp remained so fond she later published the book *Dancers on Horseback*, which offered the first history of Perry-Mansfield.

When Mary (Bunny) Hinkson stopped off at P-M with a touring dance group from the University of Wisconsin, she didn't know she would be asked to stay and teach. Hinkson studied with the Martha Graham Dance Company and at Julliard. She was the only black girl in an all-white company. Her charm and energy animated her students. While she was at P-M, she told Charlotte she wanted to be in a drama, so she was cast as the nurse in Federico García Lorca's *Blood Wedding*, the same play that Charlotte had directed a scene from for Lee Strasberg. When Bunny stood on stage, she said, "I've never spoken on the stage in all my life. Could I just move to it for a while? I'll learn the lines, but I won't speak them yet. Just let me move to them." When Hinkson finally did perform, she assumed the role perfectly, and Charlotte learned a bit about movement in acting.[135]

By 1948, the Ute Sun Dances that P-M students had been attending for so many years were slowly dying off, according to camper Shirley Ann Boutcher. From several hundred Utes dancing, the numbers had dwindled to twelve; however, the experience was still inspiring. Shortly afterward, P-M's excursions to observe Native American dances died out as well.

1949

Small rural towns often lacked decent hospitals. Steamboat was no exception. When a movement started to raise money for a new hospital, P-M held productions with proceeds going to the hospital building fund. Portia secured a special release production of the musical *Brigadoon*, which had only recently premiered in Denver. Lee Remick starred, and the play received a standing ovation. Steamboat's townspeople finally understood the value of having a camp for the arts in their town. For the campers and teachers, having a camp in the wilderness somehow allowed them to be freer, work harder and expand further. What the natural element added for those at camp was perfectly captured by camper Ann Vachon:

The most beautiful scene I ever experienced was in Colorado....The sky was doing wonderful things with its grey and blue and green, and bits of sun. Nancy Sears and I stood and waited for the rain. And it came! We ran down the roads, past the stables, through the rain. The sun left golden puddles in every leaf and the gold dripped from fences and ran down the tall grasses and splashed in our faces. The mountains had wonderful lights and shadows and in the distance everything was misty. The lovely aspens quivered in the wind; the grasses waved. And then there arched a complete rainbow and above that two smaller ones. We stood and drank the rain through every part of ourselves and felt a part of it all!

1950

In the 1950s, there were three main forms of transportation at camp: the Merry Christmas, a green truck with bright red seating in the back for campers; Blue Streak, a blue pickup truck; and the Tally Ho, a pickup truck with bench seats in back to take small groups on short outings. Those trucks transported talented actors to and from town and to the hot springs, including Ellen Holly from the New York Shakespeare Festival as an instructor, E.J. Peaker, Sammy Bayes and Joan Van Ark as students. When Peaker first tried out for the lead in *The Matchmaker*, Charlotte told her, "I'm sorry. That's not what I'm looking for." Peaker said, "Let me try it again. I *know* I can do it." At the audition were a number of male actors from the Pasadena Playhouse who thought she wouldn't be able to pull off the role, but Charlotte had a feeling about her. Peaker was given the role, and she played the part perfectly. She went on to perform on Broadway and on TV, including *Three's a Crowd* with Larry Hagman.

With E.J. came her friend Sammy Bayes. He went on to became Jerome Robbins's first man. He staged *Fiddler on the Roof* all over the world and was nominated for a Tony for his staging of *Canterbury Tales*. One night, for fun, he arranged a spontaneous faculty show in which each instructor was to become an animal. Charlotte chose a turtle, while Bayes chose a fox. "As Sammy prepared for his entrance, you could see his body turn into a fox before he leaped onto the stage in one flowing movement, causing the audience to swoon with delight and laughter. The fox then tangoed with Harriette Ann Gray, who was a snake. A snake and fox tango!" recalled Charlotte of the night.[136]

Of Joan Van Ark, Charlotte once said, "She is what a director struggles to find all her life, the kind of student who is thorough, hard working, delightful, perceptive and lots of fun to work with. She could play anything."[137] In high school, through her father's contacts at Denver's *Rocky Mountain News*, Van Ark interviewed Julie Harris. Harris advised her to apply to the Yale School of Drama at Yale University. Van Ark did and became the second-youngest student to attend the school on scholarship. Harris was the first. Van Ark ended up as the star of *Knots Landing*.

9

SQUARE DANCE FESTIVAL

1950

In the 1950s, Elizabeth Shannon, head of the equestrian department, became enamored with square dancing, the style of dance that had been such a beloved form of art in Steamboat. The craze was storming the nation. Shannon and Portia conceived of a Square Dance Festival to attract dancers to town.

Perry-Mansfield's reputation as a unique institution was enhanced with the first annual Square Dance Festival. Perry-Mansfield and Lowell Whiteman Ranch combined with the Glenwood Springs Chamber of Commerce to launch the Steamboat Springs Square Dance Festival. Dancers came from across the country to compete for awards.

The organizers were expecting a few hundred local people, but close to three thousand dancers and spectators from around the country showed up. The main road through town, Highway 40, closed for the competition. The four-day "square dance rodeo" attracted so many people that some visitors ended up sleeping in the streets. Teams were judged for technical execution, expression and enthusiasm, appearance and costume. The Stampeders from Denver took the prize. All monies raised went to the new hospital, and the event was even covered by *Newsweek*.

The first Square Dance Festival was such a huge success that they held a second one in 1951. Four thousand people attended. Ed Gilmore from Yucaipa, California, did the calling. He was said to be the best in the country. Harriette Ann Gray kicked off the festivities by riding her horse in, jumping off and

The Square Dance Festival took place on Main Street in Steamboat Springs and attracted national media attention. *Perry-Mansfield Archives.*

performing a dance. Other attractions included the Ki-wan-ii Indian Dancers, Perry-Mansfield and Lowell Whiteman Camps Junior Dancers, square dancing for children and square dancing on horseback before the day opened up for a free-for-all where everybody in attendance was invited to join in.

That evening, the Tread of Pioneers Museum put on a pageant telling the story of Routt County, beginning with the arrival of the first white man meeting with the Indians, the trapper, the prospector and finally the pioneers. The most memorable moment of the day was the pageant opener, where the Ute Indians were invited to dance. This marked the first time since the Utes were relocated from their ancestral homes in Steamboat to a reservation in Utah that they shared their dances and danced together with white folks. No one in attendance would forget that brief moment of integration.[138]

1959

By 1959, the Annual Square Dance Festival had become one of the oldest in the state. That year's festivities included a western barbeque, groups with authentic pioneer costumes and a presentation of costumed dances from the 1870s through the early 1900s. Ed Gilmore was back to do the calling, and the tradition of square dancing on horseback was continued by Elizabeth Shannon and Ken Matchett of the Gaylord-Whiteman School.[139]

10
THE 1950s

1951

After spending a winter in Mexico studying the Conchero Dancers for Portia's doctoral thesis for NYU, the ladies were surprised to find the granddaughter of the chief of the Mexican Concheros, Consuela Hernandez, on their doorstep wanting to dance. She became the first Mexican student to attend P-M.

Following her arrival were approximately 210 staff and campers. Charlotte directed *As You Like It*, the first Shakespeare play produced at camp. Fourteen members of Portia's dance company presented a ballet at the Denver Auditorium as part of a celebration dedicated to Colorado's fifty years of statehood.[140]

Once again, the winter school of P-M moved, this time to 15 West Sixty-Seventh Street in New York. The staff that year included Portia, Charlotte, Barney Brown for drama, Harriette Ann Gray, Peggy Lawler and John Wilson for dance and Helen Lanfer and Louis Horst for music. Charlotte's Hunter College Children's Theatre was to be part of the project and give performances throughout the winter. The winter school also housed Harriette Ann Gray's Dance Group, which made its New York debut that winter before heading out on a national tour.

Barney Brown. *Perry-Mansfield Archives.*

1952

Some 250 campers and staff came to P-M from New York City, British Columbia, Mexico, China and elsewhere in the United States. Units were enlarged to accommodate more campers. One of the plays performed that year was *Uncle Tom's Cabin*, which was the play Portia had first seen as a child when she snuck into the theater across the street from the hotel her father was managing.

1953

Portia earned her doctor of education degree in anthropology from New York University for her film on the Conchero Dancers of Mexico. In

Mexico, she stayed with Alice Paine Paul, a former instructor at P-M. Paul was living with the Concheros. "When she first asked if she could dance with them, they told her no. She danced for them anyway. When they saw her move as well as they could, they thought she was an angel sent from heaven to dance with them. The chief accepted her and she stayed down in Mexico with them."[141]

Portia filmed the fiestas and *peregrinaciones* in the various corners of Mexico and even convinced Charlotte to fly down and join her:

> *Portia arrived at the airport in a car filled with the chief of dancers and his wife, the queen, headdresses with feathers three feet long flying everywhere and feathered costumes....December 12th marked the annual fiesta in Mexico City where people from all over the country came. In order to get close-ups of the festivities, Portia had to join the parade. For three miles she walked with them. There were thousands of people. During the final peregrinacion, dances took place (for twelve hours)....At dawn a woman began to sing, an old woman. The song was a sad, plaintive song. The dancers stopped, took off their fancy clothes and lay down to rest. The ceremony was over. "And for that, she got a Doctor's degree," remarked Charlotte.*[142]

Portia wrote in her dissertation, "In order to have international understanding and cooperation, we need to acquire knowledge and respect for other people and their cultures, their traditions, their customs and attitudes, their social institutions, their needs and aspirations for the future. We must also learn to admit the worth of human values and the ways of living we ourselves do not accept."[143] Her thesis was considered to be one of the first accepted in film form. The films were shared with college anthropology departments across the country.

1954

Charlotte earned her master's degree in theater from New York University.[144] At the age of sixty-seven, Portia, Charlotte (sixty-five) and Helen Smith in her white gloves took a boat ride from Lily Park to Echo Park (Pat's Hole) on the Yampa River to test the waters for a new camping excursion. The Yampa River, nicknamed the "River of No Return," had first been explored only a few years prior by Buz Hatch and his assistant David Allen. The river had been considered too dangerous for exploration, with deep canyons and long, isolated stretches. With the improvements in boating equipment, river men were able to take on the challenge for the first time. In 1954, *National Geographic* magazine published Hatch and Allen's account of their journey. For some reason, Portia and Charlotte thought this might be a good addition to the summer curriculum.

After breakfast by the river, the adventurers embarked on easy waters, which later turned to whitewater. They camped under canyon walls that reached to almost two thousand feet—some overhanging—and stopped at Hell's Canyon to visit Charlie Mantle, the only settler in the canyon for a fifty-mile span. A fight between an eagle and two Canadian wild geese was a highlight. After two days, the party arrived safely at their destination.

1955

In August 1955, *Rocky Mountain News* declared P-M to be "the oldest summer school of dance in the country, their partnership the most long-lasting in all the wide world of the stage and the theater, their influence felt and exerted on nearly every phase of the entertainment world—Broadway, vaudeville, dance, education and movies."[145]

That winter, Charlotte, Portia and Helen gave up New York for good. Charlotte purchased a home back in Carmel, California, which would serve as Charlotte, Helen and Portia's winter living quarters for the rest of their lives.

1956

After initially asking Helen Smith to decline the offer for her, Charlotte accepted a position as an instructor for the drama department at the Santa Catalina School during the winter months. She went on to direct the Children's Theatre Program until her retirement at ninety-two years old.

Portia produced two new motion pictures at Perry-Mansfield, *Dance Composition as Taught in Four California Colleges* and *The Barrel*, adapted from the story of Edna St. Vincent Millay, directed by Barney Brown, music by John Wilson, choreographed by Harriette Ann Gray, danced and mimed by

Dance and theater were introduced to campers at a young age to help build their appreciation of and interest in the arts. *Perry-Mansfield Archives.*

Harriette Ann Gray and John Wilson.[146] *The Barrel* was selected a year later as one of the outstanding fifteen-millimeter films of the year at the Golden Reel Festival of the American Film Assembly.

1957

A new black box theater was built at camp at a cost of $15,000. The architect and actor Willard Sage, who studied under Frank Lloyd Wright, brought his principles to the new structure. Charlotte conceived of the design, which could serve as a proscenium, thrust or in-the-round theater and was believed to be one of the first theaters in the country to offer that type of versatility. The hexagonal building incorporated rose-colored cement and stones from the surrounding environment. The sixth side of the theater was composed of two large sliding doors and used in plays, including one in which the actors literally jumped off the stage to continue the scene in the woods outside where a real bonfire sparked and crackled and horses rode off in the distance. The theater was dedicated to Julie Harris. As part of the dedication, during sunset on the night of the unveiling, Willard Sage placed a time capsule with copies of the *Steamboat Pilot*'s articles about the building of the theater, the name of the builders and a list of people who had played important roles throughout the years at Perry-Mansfield in a cell under the fireplace.

Charlotte chose a complicated drama for the first production in the new theater: *A Bridge to the Collines Brulees*, a dramatic adaptation of Anne de Tourville's novel *Wedding Dance* that deals with superstition in the time of rural Brittany. The play utilized both the proscenium and arena stages. Daniel Nagrin, Heather MacRae (daughter of Gordon MacRae) and Maggie Howard (daughter of Broadway playwright Sidney Howard) played lead roles. The play took place over four acts with nineteen scene changes, twenty-six actors, six musicals, sixteen dancers, twenty-nine members of the production crew and Charlotte Perry directing it all. The younger actors only appeared in the first scene so they could get to bed on time.[147] The play also included an unknown actor, Dustin Hoffman.

When Portia heard hands beating on bongo drums, she went to investigate. The same notes played over and over created a backdrop for

Designed in the style of Frank Lloyd Wright, the Julie Harris Theatre blends into its surroundings. *Author's collection.*

camp that summer, as a young student named "Dusty" spent every spare moment banging his drums or noodling on the piano. Not one to pass up an opportunity to harness talent, Portia recruited him to improvise music for her modern dance class. He had a natural gift for music, even though he was at P-M to study dance. His ability to act, however, outweighed his dancing and musical skills. He spent the next two years studying with Charlotte and Barney Brown. He was the type of actor that was very particular and witty. When Helen Smith asked him if he would be coming to the opening party for the parents, he responded, "Miss Smith, I'm allergic to garden parties." He later starred in *The Graduate, Kramer vs. Kramer, Rain Man, Tootsie, Hook* and many other films, winning two Academy Awards, six Golden Globes and an Emmy. When he returned for a play in Denver and was interviewed by the press, he said, "Say hello to Portia for me."

That year's Theatre Festival included dances from Daniel Nagrin, Helen Tamaris, Harriette Ann Gray, Virginia Tanner and Jacqueline Cecil. Helen Tamaris's *Chrysalis* premiered with over thirty dancers on stage. The performance involved a girl in a Jewish family who wanted to break away from the orthodox religion. At the back of the stage she saw the world with

Swimming competitions took place at the end of summer at the bathhouse in Steamboat Springs (now the Old Town Hot Springs). *Perry-Mansfield Archives.*

all the things she might go through in life or wanted to go through. The girl danced through her conflict. Amid the toils of sensual dances, there was the solemnity and tranquility of the Passover. In the final scene, after seeing what the world had to offer, the girl threw herself into the arms of her father. The performance received rave reviews. Tamaris later credited Perry-Mansfield as being the place she created some of her best works.

To celebrate the end of summer, a Water Carnival was held. The competition and exhibition included swimmers from P-M and from the Lowell Whiteman (Boys) Camp up the road. Exhibitions included diving, water ballet and water routines. According to the *Steamboat Pilot*, the event was not to be missed.

Helen Tamaris and Dustin Hoffman. *Perry-Mansfield Archives.*

With the ladies beginning to feel their age, they needed an assistant who could run all over camp for them. When T. Ray Faulkner saw a brochure for a job that combined the outdoors and dance, she knew this was her dream job. By the time Portia responded to her application, Faulkner had taken another job. In typical Portia fashion, she asked if Faulkner would come out after her job ended to evaluate Perry-Mansfield's program. T. Ray wasn't even twenty-five years old, and she was being treated not just as an adult but also as an expert in the field of camping. She visited and accepted a job for the following year.

She began as a counselor before being asked to assist Charlotte and Portia. Mornings started with breakfast on the patio of Cabeen with hot glasses of potsam, one thin whole wheat piece of bread, a poached egg, a small glass of orange juice, canned fruit, a bowl of homemade yogurt with wheat germ poured over it and a dish filled with twelve vitamins. The day's activities were discussed and planned out. Unofficially, Ray headed all recreation activities for the camp. Officially, she did everything the ladies didn't have time to do.

T. Ray Faulkner. *Perry-Mansfield Archives.*

Ray was raised in a Baptist household where she was taught that "dancing was for whores," yet she always wanted to dance and was drawn to modern dance. At P-M, T. Ray found her tribe. She was allowed to take classes in dance when her schedule allowed. Ruthanna Boris, a soloist with the American Ballet Theatre and American Ballet Caravan, ballerina with the Metropolitan Opera and ballerina and choreographer with the Ballet Russe de Monte Carlo, once told her she moved beautifully. Portia photographed her on the tennis courts as she had done with so many other famous dancers.

1958

A separate office was built at camp. World premieres by both Helen Tamaris and Daniel Nagrin took place. Tamaris launched *Dance for Walt Whitman* and *The Vine on the Tree.* Nagrin premiered *With My Eye and with My Hand* and performed his works *Jazz, Three Ways, Indeterminate Figure* and *Three Happy Men.*[148]

After the students left that year, a mountain lion took up residence near camp. Marjorie Perry reported his presence in that winter's *Pine Bark.* She also wrote of "the coyotes' howl when the town whistle blows and the snow that glistens and icicles that drip diamonds."[149] Christmas greetings from the ladies said:

> *Merry Christmas to you who have come to Perry-Mansfield, each and every one!...We feel that you speak to us every time that you reach for honesty, awareness and precision in your art, for a shade more of understanding and creativeness in your relationships, a chance to bring new life and magic to the world around you through the rediscovery of the out-of-doors! Because this is what, by grace of you, Perry-Mansfield stood for—and, with your help, stands for today!*
>
> —*Charlotte Perry and Portia Mansfield.*

1959

In 1959, 276 counselors, maintenance men, staff and talented actors and dancers arrived from all over the world, including Mako of Japan; Tozum Uzman of Turkey; Count Bertrand de Guillin d'Avenas of France; Al Huang of Formosa; Nino Vargas of Panama; and John Patu of Samoa.

Al Hung-Liang Huang (1959–60) later became an author and founder of Living Tao Foundation. At camp, he rode horses whenever possible and

Above: Mako (*second from right*) and Al Huang (*far right*). *Perry-Mansfield Archives.*

Right: Modern dance at Perry-Mansfield. *Perry-Mansfield Archives.*

found not the west but a sense of true east. Modern dance and the essence it nurtured, for Huang, was like going back into meditation and into the old belief of what the body was. There was a recognition between the two meditations, between modern dance and tai chi meditation.[150] He later premiered *New Born* at camp, a solo that satirized the conflict between the ego of a living creature and his environment.

When he was studying at UCLA, he wrote to Charlotte: "In acting class I did the scene between Luntha and Tuptim from 'The King and I' in my voice class, and I was surprised that I found myself directing it and analyzing every little part, because last semester I had all sorts of trouble. Kingo, I've learned all that from you!"

He later remembered of the ladies, "They had the Divine Madness. They laugh at each other and they are mad sometimes but divinely mad."[151]

Mako Iwamatsu of Japan was an expert swimmer. He drove a truck and worked as a carpenter to pay for his scholarship with Harriette Ann Gray and classes with Charlotte. He later won an Academy Award nomination for his role as Po-Han in *The Sand Pebbles* and was frequently cast by Chuck Norris. He was nominated for a Tony in 1976 for his work in *Pacific Overtures* and had a role in *Seven Years in Tibet*.

After camp was officially over, P-M offered a dance seminar that included master classes in basic movement, children's creative dance, contemporary dance and advanced ballet. There was a rest period and a luncheon before mime, jazz and primitive dance. Then cars took the dancers to the Steamboat Springs Hot Mineral Pools for a swim before dinner was served. Teachers included Portia Mansfield, Harriette Ann Gray and Joey Luckie Rigsby. Rigsby had gone on from her early years as a camper to teach music and dance forms and dance composition. She studied in Florence, Italy, and toured the country as a member of the Humphrey-Weidman Dance Company. During the war, she was a civilian flight instructor for the navy.

SYMPOSIUM OF ARTS

1952–1955

In 1952, the first annual Symposium of Arts was held at P-M. The purpose was to open a dialogue about the importance of the arts in rural towns across the United States. Charlotte and Portia recognized that art can save lives, reflect the culture and times we live in and serve as a form of expression. "Recreation is, to many of us, more interesting and more effective as recreation, if it is also cultural, involving the arts. Because of this, and the confidence that many communities, remote from big cities, could have their own recreational art programs by cooperating with each other and sharing their knowledge and experience, the Symposium of Arts [was created]," wrote Portia Mansfield.[152]

For the first symposium, the mayor of Denver was in attendance. Classes were held to showcase ballet, modern dance, drama and children's dance. As part of the symposium, the very first opera was given in Steamboat by Gian Carlo Menotti, titled *Amahl and the Night Visitors*. A selection of performances by the Perry-Mansfield Camp theater was given in the evenings. Alice Paine Paul, Elizabeth Waters, Harriette Ann Gray and her dance group and Martha Wilcox all participated. Tillie Losch, ballerina turned artist, exhibited her paintings, as did P-M instructor Paul Bond and Vance Kirkland, instructor of art at Denver University. Discussions were held relating to art, music and theater.[153]

During the second Symposium of Arts, Gordon Johnston, dean of the Law School, University of Denver, who formerly acted as director of a

Perry-Mansfield is believed to be the first institute in the United States to teach both modern dance and traditional ballet under the same roof. *Perry-Mansfield Archives.*

twenty-week program for the Denver Art Museum and has also had many appearances in dramas given by local theater groups, suggested, "Man's urge for art and need to express himself, could be fulfilled by singing in the shower, putting on a Christmas pageant or building floats for a parade. Many expressions are unguided and spontaneous."[154] Portia and Charlotte noted how any organization within a community could house creative processes, including churches and schools, and that although art should maintain high standards, everyone had to start somewhere, learn from their mistakes and then continue to grow and expand. As one housewife who had organized a home orchestra put it, "Anything worth doing at all, is worth doing badly!"

The Symposium of Arts was held at P-M for four years before the ladies felt it should take place at other locations throughout Colorado. For the final year, Dr. Gordon Johnston served as the general chairman while Governor Edwin C. Johnson was the guest of honor. Panels included discussions on art, dance, music, drama, public relations and reports from community arts associations. Louise Wells, from the fine arts department of the Denver Public Library, and Ann Barzell, dance critic of the *Chicago*

Herald American, were among those of note. Music panelists included Walter Herbert, general director and conductor of the Greater Denver Opera Association, and Emma Brady Rogers, music critic of the *Rocky Mountain News*. Kathleen Horsman, a ceramicist from Edinburgh, Scotland, served as an art panelist that year.[155]

The symposiums can be summed up in a quote by Ellen Wolfe, an attendee: "Too often, pioneering in the arts seems a solitary pathway to the stars. It is gratifying to find at the symposium that others have met and conquered the many hurdles involved in pursuing our dreams....We return to our work in the allied arts with renewed vigor and new goals."[156]

After the final year at P-M, the symposiums slowly faded out, but what sparked from those gatherings was the creation of the Colorado Council on the Arts. People who attended the symposiums were later influential in creating the National Endowment for the Arts.

12
EARLY 1960s

Notable instructors in the 1960s included Josephine Taylor Kronick; Shirley Ririe; Joan Moon Armstrong, Salt Lake City Repertory Dance Company; Bob Beswick, Alwin Nikolai Dance Company; Bick Goss, Broadway; Sandra Neels, Merce Cunningham Company; Carrie Nye Cavett, Broadway; John David Keller, South Coast Repertory Theater, Costa Mesa; Dale Mackley, San Francisco State University; Shirley Genther, Urban Gateways, Chicago; and Kay Uemura Henderson, Stephens College.

Over the years, a few students would fly in by private charter or family plane. One father was surprised to find only a runway and pay phone when he landed his plane. P-M may have been a world-class institution; however, the town of Steamboat was still rustic.

In 1960, Sam Caudill of Aspen built the Louis Horst Dance Studio with three of four walls designed to move. A former student of P-M donated the money for the studio anonymously. At the dedication, Marianne Crowder gave a talk titled "Where's the Body?," which discussed "dress, deportment, dance and design and their relationship to one another from medieval days to present":

> Mrs. Crowder pointed out, the body is the medium of all good, as well as all evil, and constitutes the tangible asset we all have in common. Constant affinity was traced between architecture, costume and manners of different periods and the reflection of social trends in all of those. Slides emphasized such likeness of line as the Tudor headdress to the Tudor arch;

the Gothic spire to the tall, pointed headdress of fourteenth century women; the hoopskirt to the dome of the palace of Queen Victoria's day; the lush curves of 1890 in edifices and furnishings to the corseted female; and the boyish figure of 1925 to the Empire State Building.[157]

The Perry-Mansfield Dancers then offered up dances throughout the ages.

One of the dancers, Kay Uemura (Henderson), was attending camp for the first time. When Uemura was teaching elementary school children in San Jose, taking classes and performing, she met Peggy Lawler. Lawler was dancing in Harriette Ann Gray's company and had been at Perry-Mansfield for years. She offered Uemura a scholarship for the summer of 1960 and asked her to come early to help open camp. Uemura said, "Of course." When she arrived in Steamboat at 4:30 a.m. and saw the sun rise over Strawberry Park, she thought she was in a fairyland. Evenings were filled

The Louis Horst Studio features an open-air design. Another memorable feature is the lack of mirrors to promote self-awareness and awareness within a group. *Perry-Mansfield Archives.*

Kay Henderson (*center*). *Perry-Mansfield Archives.*

with reading plays, talking and rehearsing. Throughout the summer, she would pinch herself and ask, "Is this really real? Am I dreaming?"[158]

To pay off her scholarship, Uemura worked in the kitchen. She set up conga lines to clear plates and sang her way through her work. She made kitchen duty so much fun that people not assigned to work in the kitchen joined in. Anytime she was asked to help someone out or pick up more responsibilities, she answered, "Of course." When she told Portia she was going to be married, Portia insisted that Uemura be married at P-M. She and her husband, Don Henderson, were the first couple to have their wedding on Perry-Mansfield grounds. When Portia asked her to teach on her wedding day because Harriette Ann Gray had been delayed, Kay answered, "Of course." Other staff and campers rallied together to set up a wedding filled with wildflowers and an ornate wedding cake. The ceremony was perfect. Charlotte gave the newlyweds a night in her home in town along with America's cooking services.

1961

Charlotte produced another local story, *The Cabin at Medicine Springs*, to premiere at the Perry-Mansfield Theatre Festival. Tickets for the play sold out despite being in competition with *Gone with the Wind*, which was showing locally. The play was based on the book by Lulita Crawford Pritchett, the granddaughter of the founding family of Steamboat Springs. Pritchett consulted with Perry on the play, which told the story of the Crawfords' first years in Steamboat. A favorite line of the play was "Ain't no sugar. Take some salt!" which is what Mrs. Crawford told the Ute Indians when they showed up on her door and the sugar supplies hadn't yet made it over the treacherous passes from Denver. That Charlotte's plays turned out such large audiences is a testament to her talents.

1962

Jim Edmondson. *Perry-Mansfield Archives.*

Jim Edmondson would later write to Charlotte and Portia of his time spent at P-M in 1962:

Know I've perhaps said this before; but you people have been the greatest influence on my life aside from my parents. Thank you. I will always miss and long for that world which you provided for us so many years.... The summer was a fine experience. I was amazed at how much I have been needing to act and what a fine acting teacher life and living are. Directing has become the major creative love in my life over the past few years. When it is successful I know I owe it to Kingo's influence and teaching.

122

Edmondson went on to become resident director and actor with the Oregon Shakespeare Festival and directed for the American Conservatory Theater.

1963

For the fiftieth year of camp, staff included Charlotte Perry; Dale Mackley; Melvin Davidson; Ingrid Wekerle, PhD; Nancy Kellner (aka Rusty DeLucia); Harriette Ann Gray; Joey Luckie Rigsby; Kay Uemura; Ruthanna Boris; Elizabeth Shannon; Bob Oliphant for folk dance; Georgia Jones for ballet; Josephine Taylor for children's creative dance; Portia Mansfield; Gene Perrine; Bob Skiles for art; Jim Edmundson for stage production; and Lois McElroy for costuming. The curriculum still boasted a blend of art, spirit and soul closely connected to the world around them.

Harriette Ann Gray. *Perry-Mansfield Archives.*

Ruthanna Boris had a hip ailment that ended her dance career. She stayed in a cabin that was west of the main studio. Before her class began, she dragged her bad leg to the kitchen, where one of the cooks opened the oven door. She stood in front of the heat and rubbed and rubbed her leg before walking over to the main studio, still dragging her leg every inch of the way. When she got to the studio, she stood in a beautiful first position and said, "Girls, we are ready to dance." For the hour that she taught, she did not have a limp at all. As soon as class ended, she slid her leg all the way back to her cabin.[159]

Camp also welcomed its youngest camper, Cynthia Rand, Doc Ballentine's daughter. Doc Ballentine served as assistant to the ladies for many years and always inspired the campers to give back to the world around them through charitable acts.

For the fiftieth anniversary, those involved in camp wanted to present the ladies with something to acknowledge all the lives they had touched. Bob Skiles thought of a rock. Leslie, the maintenance man, scoured the hills of Steamboat that summer to find something fitting. When he spied the rose granite, he knew this was what he was looking for, "a rock that had borne the test of time, that had sprouted from the Ice Age itself and rolled to its final resting place in Colorado."[160]

On the last day of camp, August 19, 1963, a fiesta took place. Awards and certificates were distributed to campers and counselors. Charlotte announced that the camp had been sold to Stephens College, and she spoke positively of the change:

> *The essentials of Perry-Mansfield, we are confident, will remain the same; an absorption in art with heart and mind; a sense of the close brotherhood of the arts, and of the values of a way of life close to creatures and mountains and out-of-doors. And a certain feeling will endure, too, compounded with a measure of wildness and of the special auras of a school with Perry-Mansfield's activities. One resulting from the sound of horses' hoofs on camp roads and of dancers' feet answering to music or drum beats; of conversations by children and chipmunks above Soda Creek; of the light behind Storm Mountain and on the faces of actors, of dancers, of young riders making their first low jumps in the ring; the smell of wet sage, of coffee on the porch of the Julie Harris Theatre...and of bubbling glue in the workshop, the effluvia of an out-of-the-way, unhandy, improbably entirely logical haven of the arts of young people on the Western Slope.*[161]

As a gift to P-M, Harriette Ann Gray choreographed a dance sequence titled *Celebration* to accompany Portia's films of P-M playing in the background. The evening of dance also featured Robert Kuykendall's compositions and Ruthanna Boris's ballet. At the end of the performances, Charlotte and Portia came out to a standing ovation.

The directors were then led to the aspen grove between the Julie Harris Theatre and the Louis Horst Studio. The rose-colored granite stone had been arranged with stone benches. It was joked the rock might be even older than the directors. Upon the glacier was a plaque that read:

> *In honor of the Fiftieth Anniversary of Perry-Mansfield, we of the student body, the staff and faculty, join together to create this place apart. It is intended for repose and study, to rehearse a scene, meet a friend, or just to enjoy the Colorado green.*
>
> *Whatever its use we know that all who come will think especially of Kingo and Portia and their long years of devotion to the continual growth of this school and camp....Here we have been given great opportunities and*

Charlotte Perry (*center*) and Ingrid Wekerle (*left*) relax during a rare free moment. *Perry-Mansfield Archives.*

lasting inspiration in the fine arts, in the art of living and in the continuum of these arts. When we leave we will remember, echoing Robert Frost:
"These woods are lovely, dark and deep,
But we have promises to keep
And miles to go before we sleep."

With our deep love and gratitude we dedicate this Place.

Charlotte responded:

Nothing could so have surprised us and satisfied us as a symbol of our perseverance at Perry-Mansfield than this beautiful half-hidden shrine in the crannied wall of our often frantic though always exciting life with younger and younger generations. To have a place at Camp where it is legitimate to rest, to loiter, even to think, is a curiosity, a luxury and a challenge—and the provision of it shows the most sensitive and creative imagination on the part of you who accomplished it.

Moved and grateful, we promise that we shall not wait to be born again to realize the purpose of this haven, to know that we do not have to tear past it but can divinely drop into it to prepare a class, read a play with you, listen to a joke, or look at a drawing of horses, dancers, or stage sets. From our hearts we thank you for days and days ahead, for Indian Summer twilights and for nights when we can conceivably lie on our backs on this ancient glacial rock and think on the stars.[162]

After the dedication, the party began. Portia, dressed in a special gown made for her by the costumers that year, was surrounded by her dancing students, who moved softly before her as she danced a waltz with one of the instructors.

13

STEPHENS COLLEGE

Portia and Helen Smith approached several universities to gauge their interest in taking over Perry-Mansfield. They were turned down by every one because the institutions felt the expense of running a program off-site would adversely affect the financial viability of their institution. Eventually, they turned to Stephens College.

The relationship between Stephens and P-M went back to Harriette Ann Gray, who was an instructor at both institutions. The similarities in goals of the two made Stephens an enticing organization to take the reins of P-M.[163] Charlotte and Portia agreed that P-M would be given to Stephens for ten dollars as long as Stephens ran the program to include dance, drama, the arts and the equestrian program until the ladies' deaths. At that time, they could develop the camp any way they liked. Stephens agreed. The ladies would turn over camp at the end of their fiftieth year but stay on for four years to help transition the organization.

As the transfer date closed in, Stephens became nervous that it wouldn't be able to make any money from the camp, so Portia told them, "I'll show you how to do it." She doubled her efforts at recruitment, overflowing the children's camp to a point where they had to borrow housing from the Perry family and neighboring ranches just to give everyone a place to sleep. That year boasted four hundred campers in attendance.[164] Portia also continued to bring in world-class dance instructors from around the world like Amala Shankar, who taught Indian dance with a modern flair.

In 1964, the name of camp was changed to Perry-Mansfield School and Campus of Stephens College. In order to leave camp with the flavor in

Portia's travels around the world inspired and influenced her choreography and dances. *Perry-Mansfield Archives.*

which it had existed over the past fifty years, the ladies left items that had been given as gifts, including an East Indian door hanging, Haitian drums, a Tibetan small drum, hand-printed tablecloths, an East Indian painting of Central City by Vance Kirkland, a Greek cow bell, opium pipes (antiques), a reindeer rattle, a framed Japanese cloth scene, Guatemalan drums, Danish pottery birds, Javanese shadow puppets, a dagger and holster (antique), eight painted Mexican woven-bottom chairs, a green Scotch plaid steamer rug, a Japanese hand-embroidered wall hanging, an Eskimo drum, native drums, a primitive picture, a piano and bench, a skin table, egg cups, wooden crosses, a hand-woven Italian chest cover, alabaster vases, a small Chinese vase and a green glass Mexican Madonna bottle.

They took with them two Kashmir coverlets (red on white background, about five by seven feet); eight Guatemalan hand-woven curtains; two red and white Navajo blankets; one red, white and orange antique Navajo blanket; one Holstein cowhide; one elk head; one yellow glass vase; one large heavy iron kettle; one Dutch oven; and all Navajo rugs in the entire camp.

The buildings, in much need of repair, were updated with new windows and foundations. New buildings were erected and old ones re-sided. After one student sat up in his bunk bed and got a nail in his eye, the interiors were inspected and made safer. New buildings were added, including Aspen (1977), Spruce (1978), Willow, Sagebrush and Woodshack (1979), the Art Department addition to main lodge (1980), Pine and Kinnikinnik (1980), Tractor Shed (1983) and Conrad Hall (1985).

Stainless steel counters were put in the kitchen, along with a dishwasher and convection oven to satisfy the health department. In 1967, storms brought down trees that crushed one of the cabins and took out electrical wires, which had to be repaired and replaced. Over the past fifty years, the water system had been patched together with tape and glue. Stephens installed a twenty-thousand-gallon underground water tank and replaced all the water lines. The electrical system was trenched underground, and all buildings were given new entry conduits and service boxes. All in all, Stephens invested $500,000 into renovating the camp.[165]

Stephens also expanded the paths from one place to another on campus. Trees were cut down, and the dense brush and grasses that kept the place feeling wild were cut away to comply with fire safety restrictions. When Portia returned one summer to walk through campus with her friend Dorothy Wither, Wither asked, "Isn't it sad they have cut down so many trees?" Portia responded, "Yes, but think of all the little plants that are now free to feel the sun."[166]

Inevitably, camp changed. Harriette Ann Gray and Kay Uemura upheld the dance program to the same acclaim as in the past. Martha Nishitani remembers attending Perry-Mansfield in 1965. She cooked breakfast for four hundred campers, danced till noon, helped cook lunch for the campers, danced till bedtime and still found time to date one of the local boys of Steamboat. In 1951, Nishitani established her own dance company, and by 1959, she was recognized throughout Seattle for her modern dance.

Like Perry-Mansfield, Stephens believed that students learned and matured best from a variety of experiences. Writing classes were added to the program. Whitewater rafting trips and wilderness backpacking were revived. Music classes were offered. Horsemanship continued, although when Stephens didn't have the money to bring horses out one year for the summer program, Elizabeth Shannon paid out of her own pocket to keep the equestrian program running and to feed the horses that year.

Randy Nelson, the program director, approached DeLucia to start a pre-camp program, called Discovery Camp, which would involve the Steamboat Springs children. At the inception of the program, the children took five classes in the morning in the fine arts (theater, dance, creative writing, music and art), and in the afternoons, they had camp activities that included horseback riding or trips to town and the local hot springs. In her classes, which she still teaches at P-M today, DeLucia keeps Charlotte's spirit alive in the children's theater department. She tells them, "If you don't believe it yourself then it won't come across on stage."

The one program that faltered was the theater program for high school and college students. Theater classes became electives instead of one of the main programs at camp because Stephens had a separate theater camp for its students. Those attending P-M during those years were there for dance.

Beginning in the early 1970s, enrollment dropped. Camp was operating in the red. Decisions had to be made as to whether or not Stephens should keep Perry-Mansfield. Stephens's new president, Arland Chris-Juaco, took a trip to P-M to evaluate the

Top right: Elizabeth Shannon. *Perry-Mansfield Archives.*

Above: Dancers leap into the air in the 1940s. *Perry-Mansfield Archives.*

program. He felt magic in Perry-Mansfield and continued funds to improve the camp.[167] Five log cabins were added in order to be rented through the summers and winters to help increase revenue. By 1978, P-M was operating in the black again. In the 1980s, while enrollment was finally growing at Perry-Mansfield, enrollment was falling at Stephens's main campus. Arland Chris-Juaco was replaced by Patsy Sampson. The new president reviewed the school's finances and decided Perry-Mansfield had to be sold. "Our overriding reason for moving the P-M program to Columbia is that we want to offer the best dance program we can. We are a small college. We must consolidate and focus our resources to do that," Sampson said.[168]

Her decision was not made lightly, knowing how attached students and instructors were to the institution. The property, however, sat in a now-developed and exclusive section of Steamboat Springs, which, if sold, could bring in a significant amount of revenue for Stephens. The decision was made that P-M would be sold not as a camp but as a real estate holding.

14

FRIENDS OF PERRY-MANSFIELD

Stephens made the announcement during the 1990 season that it would not run camp the following year but that the school was not going to put camp on the market—yet. According to theater instructor Bruce Roach, "Anyone who had any relationship with camp in the past and those of us who were there that summer were up in arms over Stephens's decision to sell because we were afraid it was going to be sold off to developers." Noel Hefty and Holly Williams began to brainstorm a way to save Perry-Mansfield. They reached out to the community through an ad in the paper to see what kind of support the mission to save Perry-Mansfield might generate. From the group that showed up at the first meeting, Friends of Perry-Mansfield was born. Randy Nelson, program director from the Stephens years at P-M, drove out to Steamboat to offer his services to keep camp running the following year. With a director in place, in September 1990, Noel Hefty got on a plane for Missouri. She met with President Patsy Sampson and offered one dollar to let the Friends run the program the following year so that camp's doors wouldn't close. Hefty also presented the first right of refusal should the Board of Regents choose to sell. Stephens accepted. In the spring of 1991, the Board of Regents announced its decision to sell P-M.

When students at Stephens's main campus heard P-M was to be sold, protests sprang up. Students marched with signs saying "Save Perry-Mansfield: Keep Art Alive," "Art Has No Price" and "Dance + Dreams = Perry-Mansfield."[169] Students wore protest pins that read "Save Art, Save History, Save Nature, Save Tradition, Save Excellence, Save Theatre.

Save Stephens/Perry-Mansfield." Nina LaMetterey shared many students' sentiments when she wrote, "I have learned at Perry-Mansfield. I have grown there, loved there, laughed there and cried there. Most of all I have felt like *somebody* there. It's probably the only place where I have lived where I feel as if I belong."

Interest in owning the land was immediate and included a news anchor in a fur coat who wanted to turn the camp into a vacation retreat for his family, as well as developers. In order to be taken seriously at the negotiation table for a first right of refusal, Stephens asked Friends of Perry-Mansfield to come up with 10 percent of the $1.2 million asking price, a steep increase over the $10.00 Stephens paid for the camp.

Friends of P-M sprang into action. Local support was overwhelming. Once foundations throughout Colorado understood the community was behind the effort, they began giving donations as well. Friends used every means they could to get the word out that camp was to be sold and were successful in gaining coverage on NBC. Roger O'Neil ran a segment on his Sunday morning program titled *Pas de Dough*, a play on the dance term *pas de deux*. The segment talked about the struggles of small colleges and P-M's place as a national treasure. Deborah Jowitt, dance critic for the *Village Voice*, wrote an article about saving P-M that became the cover story for *Dance Magazine*. People called asking, "How can I help?"

Friends had no startup money for marketing, recruiting or paying staff that first year. Holly Williams approached the Steamboat Springs City Council and requested a loan, which she received. Friends knew if they couldn't break even their first year of camp they wouldn't be able to afford to keep running the camp in the long run. Sammy Bayes offered a master class for the summer of 1991 that drew a lot of publicity and campers. Laurie Gamache, the final Broadway Cassie in the original production of *A Chorus Line*, taught that year. Joan van Ark, Julie Harris, E.J. Peaker, Scott Benson, Shirley Ririe, Kat Knapp and Alice Oakes-McMahon all offered to help.

Several instructors remained through the transition, including Michael Kelly Bruce in dance and Bruce Roach in theater. All in all, Michael Kelly Bruce spent close to twenty-eight summers at camp from camper to teacher. The first year he stepped foot on P-M grounds, he thought he was going to major in film. As part of the course requirements, theater students also had to take dance. He skipped the first dance class because he and his friends didn't want to put on the black tights they were required to wear. The next day, they were told they had to go to dance class, so they did. Harriette Ann

Michael Kelly Bruce. *Perry-Mansfield Archives.*

Gray was his teacher, and he was hooked, entering a long career in dance and choreography.[170]

Bruce Roach, an established actor, had been recruited by Nina Cochran to teach in the summer of 1990. He had never taught or directed before, but Cochran told him, "I have a feeling you would be really good for this place and this place would be really good for you."[171] Roach returned to camp for eleven seasons, along with instructors from around the world. His time at camp "changed my life." Today, he continues to teach an actor training program at the University of Minnesota in partnership with the Guthrie Theatre.

Randy Nelson oversaw the summer program, and Randy, Nina Cochran and Laura LaMetterey managed camp. At the end of the year, financially, camp was a success. Williams recalled thinking, "We can keep this going."

With that mindset, the next step was to purchase camp from Stephens. Bob Weiss, a lawyer in Steamboat who had been connected to P-M for many years, was essential for getting the camp under contract, handling purchase agreements and more. P-M Board member Jack Morrison, a local realtor, and John Kerst, who worked in banking for over twenty years and who later went on to be awarded the Steamboat Springs Heritage Award for his philanthropic work throughout the years, helped negotiate the purchase from Stephens.

Over the next three years, through an outpouring of support in Steamboat, from foundations across Colorado and even national aid, Stephens was paid off, and then the mortgage—taken out to help finance the payments—was finally paid off completely in 1994. Friends owned camp outright. A mortgage-burning party was held to celebrate. A small log structure that looked like a miniature bonfire was built inside the Julie Harris Theatre, as there was a fire restriction in Routt County that prevented an outdoor bonfire. Everyone who attended the burning of the mortgage was given a pen to write a note to be placed on the fire. As the past burned, the ashes made way for a new chapter in Perry-Mansfield's history. To conclude the celebration, a gospel choir and approximately 350 people in attendance sang "Amazing Grace" as dancers spun on the lawn. Then Nina Cochran sang an original rendition of "This Land Is Your Land."

In 1994, P-M was placed in the National Register of Historic Places. "Since 1994 the Perry-Mansfield Performing Arts School and Camp has received more than $920,000 in preservation grants from the History Colorado State Historical Fund for interior and exterior restoration and rehabilitation, stabilization, and planning."[172] Scene Shop was built in 1996 when it was noticed backdrops were being built in the rain with no shelter. At the time Friends took over, Marjorie Perry's cabin and the Upper Perry Cabin that bordered camp remained part of the Perry family estate—until 2012, when the property was sold. Miraculously, P-M was later able to acquire the property with most of Marjorie Perry's belongings still intact.

In 1995, in order to show supporters that Perry-Mansfield was here to stay, the Steinberg Pavilion was conceived. The dance studio was designed by Joe Robbins and built by Snake River Construction to reflect Frank Lloyd Wright's concept of prairie structures that was incorporated into both the Julie Harris Theatre and the Louis Horst Dance Studio but on a larger scale. The pavilion became the first year-round facility for dance rehearsals. The building's glass doors let the outside in while reflecting its environment through small details, such as aspens on the beams. The Steinberg Pavilion was funded by the Harold and Mimi Steinberg Charitable Trust and was dedicated in 1997.

With Friends in charge, a renaissance of the early days of P-M began. Perry-Mansfield renewed its ties to Julliard in 2000, with Linda Kent heading the dance program for fourteen years and Jennifer Golonka as an instructor and recruiter for twelve of those years. Kent was the principal dancer for

"We are here to stay." The Steinberg Pavilion was built after Friends of Perry-Mansfield purchased the camp from Stephens College. The purpose of the building was to let the community and alumni know that Perry-Mansfield would be around for many more years. *Author's collection.*

the Alvin Ailey American Dance Theater from 1968 to 1974 and the only white dancer accepted. She was also the principal dancer for the Paul Taylor Dance Company from 1975 to 1989. Under Kent's tutelage, connections were renewed with the Alvin Ailey Company and the Paul Taylor Company. The dancers Perry-Mansfield attracted were some of the most talented to ever attend camp. Performance Camp, an intensive program for pre-professionals, was instituted. Noel Hefty, with her background in dance, auditioned and recruited dancers. Hefty and her husband, Terry Hefty, also sponsor scholarships for dancers. "Terry and I have always believed that if we could change one person's life then we have fulfilled our intent for all the scholarships we give." They have affected far more than one person's life. Sarah Tallman received a scholarship from the Heftys and has gone on to dance with David Taylor Dance Theatre and Gleich Dancers Contemporary Ballet, has been a principal artist with Central City Opera and is in her eleventh season with Wonderbound.[173] On an annual basis, fifteen to twenty-five students receive some amount of scholarship money from the Heftys to attend P-M. "It's amazing how many thank-you notes I receive with the expression, 'Perry-Mansfield changed my life,'" said Noel Hefty.

In 2016, a ten-day intensive pre-professional program was offered to give students a taste of what it would be like to be in a small dance company because there are few fifty-two- and thirty-four-week contracts anymore. The program was developed by the new co-directors of the dance program, husband-and-wife team Christopher Compton and Tammy Dyke-Compton. "It's a taste of what it would be like to be hired by a private choreographer like Stacey Tookey, of *So You Think You Can Dance* fame," said Dyke-Compton. Tookey was chosen as the artist-in-residence for 2016, which was also an opportunity for Tookey and her company, Still Motion Dance Company, to create a show and produce the art they want to produce with no restrictions. "Being at P-M gave her a lot of freedom and inspiration to create with the artists she wants to work with," said Tammy Dyke-Compton. Dyke-Compton first came to P-M when she was sixteen and given a scholarship. At camp, she was first introduced to modern dance. She had no idea what concert dance was, and this was her first summer on her own away from family. She was set to stay for six weeks but was invited to stay two additional weeks. Other students from the Julliard School told her she should apply to study there. She had never heard of Julliard before but took their advice, auditioning with a solo dance choreographed for her by Michael Kelly Bruce during her summer at P-M. She was accepted. Linda Kent was her teacher at Julliard at the same time Kent was the director of the Dance Department at P-M and hired her as a teacher for P-M. Now she serves as co-director.

As for her husband, although he is also a dancer, he first came to P-M as a security guard in the evenings so he could take care of their son during the day while Dyke-Compton taught. He and Kent hit it off, and he ended up teaching partnering and repertory classes with her that summer. Eight years later, his phone is ringing every thirty seconds as they start working on the program for next year.

Once again, Perry-Mansfield is an internationally recognized name in the dance community. The same is true for the theater department, which had to reinvent itself after Stephens's ownership. Because Stephens's focus was on dance, the theater classes became adjunct classes like creative writing classes to supplement the dancers' experiences in the summer. The summer of 1990—with Nina and Randy Cochran heading the theater program—things began to shift. Nina Cochran wanted a bigger experience for her students and began to change the program. When Friends took over, the theater program was once again given a place of prominence in the P-M curriculum. In the 1990s, attendance for the theater program overtook the dance program.[174] Bruce Roach and Nina Cochran developed

Welcome to Perry-Mansfield. *Perry-Mansfield Archives.*

a conservatory-style program that included different elements in acting, such as a combination voice and movement program that was team taught. Students were recruited for camp from across the country, including New York City, the state of Texas, Kansas City and San Francisco. Once again, different disciplines began to collaborate. "I had been an actor all my life and I had never had the chance to work alongside artists from other disciplines. And so every day to be living, eating and working alongside choreographers, professional musicians, visual artists and to share the entire camp experience with them was remarkable. The exchange of ideas was a transformational experience for me. My own work grew exponentially from going out there every summer," said Roach.

One of the collaborations of that time that is still talked about today is the production of *Sweeney Todd.* Jim Steinberg, festival producer for New Works Festival, said *Sweeney Todd* was "as good as anything I've seen professionally." The production came about when Rob Schiffmann, the musical director, asked Roach, "'What do you want to do that you don't think you can do?' *Sweeney Todd* was one of those things. Everyone asked 'How can you possibly do that at camp?' P-M stretched its resources and used the Julie Harris Theatre in ways it had never been used before, but it also challenged everybody involved, including the dance department, theater department and music department."[175]

Another change was that an extended program was offered at the end of the traditional six weeks of camp, called Performance Camp, where professionals worked alongside selected students for a professional production that was open to the townspeople. They also developed a New Noises program in which playwrights were invited for a residency to work with professional and student actors. The first play was *The Immaculate Conception of Malfie Dibbs* by Burgess Clark in 1998.[176] The New Plays program, now called the New Works Festival, has transformed into a traditional professional developmental program in which crews of directors, writers, dramaturges and actors come in for a week to work. Much of what happens at P-M goes on to be produced throughout the country, or as Jim Steinberg, previous executive director of the festival and current producer of the festival, says, "We have helped writers and seen works that have gone from page to stage. That's the ultimate test to me. Does it get produced and does it have subsequent productions?"

Lydia, by playwright Octavio Solis, premiered at P-M and went on to be produced throughout the country. Adam Bock, a playwright from Canada, had never had a play produced in the United States. He worked on *The Receptionist* at P-M, and it was picked up by the Manhattan Theatre Club, was written up in the *New York Times* and has been produced regularly ever since. One new feature of the theater department is that guest artists—playwrights, directors and actors—are invited to stay as guest artists for the first week of the theater program.

The year 2013 marked the centennial of P-M as a performing arts camp. One hundred years have passed since Portia and Charlotte first welcomed students to their dance camp at Lake Eldora, Colorado, where they danced under the crashing of thunder and let their bare feet skip and frolic through the grasses. Fifty years have passed without Charlotte and Portia, where like a teenager, the camp grew to independence, awkward, perhaps at first, and then like so many campers who had come to Perry-Mansfield, finally finding itself again. For the centennial celebration, Linda Kent took the stage with her summer dancers. The theater program, headed by Raelle Myrick-Hodges, co-founder of Azuka Theater in Philadelphia, helped the students direct a tribute to the ladies, which included a portion of the performance being staged outdoors in the aspen grove where the glacial rock dedicated to Portia and Charlotte served as a backdrop.

As P-M enters the next one hundred years, under Executive Director Nancy Engelken, an emphasis is once again being placed on community outreach to ensure P-M remains embedded in the local community and welcomes students from Steamboat. The program continues to grow

A dancer poses during the first year of Rocky Mountain Dance Camp. *Perry-Mansfield Archives.*

and attract cutting-edge teachers and students. At the same time P-M is reaching out locally, Engelken is building a national name for P-M through grants and marketing efforts. Due to Engelken's dedication, P-M received its first National Endowment of the Arts grant in 2016. The archives, under Karolynn Lestrud, are being preserved so the history of P-M will be remembered into the future.

Today, students still wake up in their cabins, without heat, to walk down the hill to shower because there are no bathrooms in the cabins. They eat when it's time to eat, and in between classes, they walk through a maze of wildflowers and aspens. Days are filled with dance, theater, music, drawing, painting and riding horses. "If one allows complete immersion in Perry-Mansfield, new connections will form not only with other students but with the faculty as well. Teachers are with campers 24/7. At this camp alone, one can walk up and down the paths and watch rehearsals every night as the light and the music and the sound of creation surround you. Don't worry about if you can afford it, don't worry about whether it can be done or not. What is your dream? What can you imagine?" asked Joan Lazarus, executive director during the centennial year of camp, of the next generation of P-M campers.[177] That is the Perry-Mansfield of the next one hundred years.

15

PORTIA AND CHARLOTTE AFTER PERRY-MANSFIELD

During the last years of owning P-M, Portia began to travel around the world with her sister, Margery. She visited Kathmandu, Nepal; Benares, India; Kyoto, Japan; Baghdad and Babylon, Iraq; Beirut, Lebanon; Istanbul; Rome; London; Isfahan, Iran; and Greece.

In 1966, Portia came down with an illness that left her "moving my age." In typical Portia manner, she used the opportunity to create a program of exercises for women over fifty-five. The exercises were designed to help women avoid common postural tendencies that come with age, such as protruding abdomen, beginning "dowager's hump," forward head carriage, fallen arches, sagging throat muscles and shortened hamstrings.[178]

That same year, Portia and Helen Smith opened Perry-Mansfield Boys Camp, where they served as co-directors. Portia was seventy-nine years old. Ray Palmer was the associate director and David O'Hern his assistant. Palmer brought experience from the Los Angeles County Outdoor School, where he owned and operated a mountaineering guide service in the Sierras. Elizabeth Shannon was both supervisor and teacher of riding at the boys' camp and P-M. Camp was hosted at the Lowell Whiteman ranch. Lowell Whiteman had been a camper at P-M many years prior and remained connected to Portia and Charlotte.

The program was initially designed for boys nine to sixteen and included instruction in English, western and bareback riding; hiking and learning about flora, fauna and geology; swimming; astronomy; and more. On camping trips, they carried and cooked their own food. They were encouraged to interact with the environment and build forts and bridges and different kinds of dams, and through it all, they learned problem-solving, teamwork and cooperation. They learned about the land and they learned how to take care of themselves.

Unfortunately, financially, the camp was not successful. Portia did not have the same energy she did when she was younger to travel the country to recruit campers. Yet the campers they did have were greatly influenced by their experiences. Camper Tom Martin wrote from San Francisco:

> *I have been doing a lot of climbing, every weekend in fact, and have been on several backpacking expeditions....My current interests in climbing and back-packing were begun, nurtured through some trying times and brought to completion solely under the influence of Perry-Mansfield* [Boys Camp]. *A year ago, I couldn't see myself even in my nuttiest dreams doing the kind of things I do now. And for that you all have my eternal gratitude.*

As the program progressed, canoeing, river rafting, rock and snow climbing and mountaineering were added. An expedition program for boys fifteen and up was offered to hone in on wilderness skills. Unfortunately, the program never really took off, and Palmer lost interest.[179] Portia took over and ran the program on her own for a few years. She called the boys her "summer sons."

After retiring from Perry-Mansfield, Portia Mansfield traveled the world several times over with her sister. *Perry-Mansfield Archives.*

Due to the long hours involved in running the boys' camp, often ten hours a day, even through the winter, Portia stopped dancing. She coordinated the instructors, hired staff and recruited campers. At the height of camp, approximately forty boys enrolled each summer. Those who earned their certificates went on to teach outdoor education. Girls were eventually invited to the more advanced outdoor education programs, which included rock climbing and mountaineering.

For the tenth anniversary, they set up base camp at Mica Basin, surrounded by the jagged peak of Mount Agnes in the Mount Zirkel Wilderness. Students learned rock climbing, snow climbing, expedition strategies, survival, backpacking and camping, orienteering and canoeing. Certificates were earned, valid for two years, for those who completed the course. With certification, students were invited to participate in mountaineering tours that traveled to the Snake River or Teton National Park.

Snowball fights were had in summer, flowers sampled (and not always appreciated) and fish caught. As with any outdoor expeditions, the tales of death were vivid and frequent. One young camper remembered his hike as "terrible because I was almost killed." Climbing Rabbit Ears in thunder and lightning, five guys "almost died of fright, while others got lost." One boy fell out of his river raft and thought that was the end. Another camper remembers a pack trip gleefully as "Very fun. My horse was practically killed by other horses. Ed caught a chipmunk. Went to Gold Lake."[180]

Because of the unique nature of the camp at the time, Portia felt their activities should be filmed. Even though Portia's films had earned worldwide acclaim, she had lost confidence in her ability as a filmmaker, so she reached

Campers play in snow on an outing to the high country above the town of Steamboat Springs. *Perry-Mansfield Archives.*

out to Len Aitken, who had previously filmed a kayaking expedition. He came and shot the mountaineering activities of the boys in the Wind River Range and titled the movie *The Ground Below*. The fourteen-minute color film was then sent across the country and around the world. The movie was entered into the International Festival of Films for Young Adults in Tehran, Iran, in November 1972 under the patronage of her Imperial Highness Farah Pahlavi, Empress of Iran, and was organized by the Institute for the Intellectual Development of Children and Young Adults in Iran. After seeing the film, the Empress herself wrote a note to Portia saying how impressed she was with the movie. *The Ground Below* won a 1972 CINE Golden Eagle grant for foreign distribution.

Despite these successes, camp kept losing money every year. Neither Portia nor Helen received salaries. Eventually, Bob Weiss took over. Portia retired from the camp in 1974 but remained as a consultant for the next few years. Eventually, due to financial reasons, the camp closed.

In 1969, Portia was awarded the American Camping Association Honor Award, which came with a letter from Ernest F. Schmidt, executive vice president of the American Camping Association. "I certainly want to personally congratulate you on this high honor—and at the same time express my appreciation for all you have done for camping and for children over the years." She was later awarded the Governor's Award by Governor Love in Aspen for her contributions to the state of Colorado. "Portia has brought to the people of Colorado a renewed and renewing appreciation of the art of the dance, and whereas her ability to stimulate creativity in others and her awareness of beauty both in her own field of artistic endeavor and those of others have rendered her a memorable Coloradoan," wrote Governor Love. In 2004, she was inducted into the Colorado Women's Hall of Fame.

On Valentine's Day 1974, Portia wrote that she would like to volunteer her remaining energies to help legalize euthanasia and demonstrate that ages seventy to eighty-five or more can be the best years of a person's life. In 1978, Portia wrote in a letter to her friend Carol Gossard, "Oh how fast the hours, days and weeks are flying by—and I have done so little....Whee its good to be alive. I do believe these are the best years. I don't feel like an 'old lady' tho I admit I am in years."

A year later, Portia passed away from pneumonia related to a broken hip. It is said that at the exact hour Portia passed away, the movie *A Divine Madness* by Len Aitken was completed. The movie captured the lives of Portia and Charlotte and those who had been affected by them through the years. Portia had seen an earlier cut of the film. Her life and her legacy were complete. Of her passing, Charlotte wrote to Gossard, "Now what a great hole is left here. Though I know Portia like this bird [a seagull on the writing paper] is soaring above us into a new life of great challenges, I can't help feeling lost for awhile."[181]

Charlotte had also had a full life. During her time in Chicago and during the first fifty years of Perry-Mansfield, she had been a student of Alexander Saslavsky, who was a concert violinist and concertmeister of the New York Symphony Society. She studied with Lee Strasberg, founder of the Actor's Studio in New York, Russian director Erwin Piscator and Maria Ouspenskaya. She studied with Sandy Meisner at the Neighborhood Playhouse, took theater history with John Gassner and learned playwriting at Columbia University under Arnold Sundgaard. She learned stage design and dynamic symmetry at Parsons School of Fine and Applied Art in New York City, and psychology and education were taken at the New York School of Social Work under Doctors Kenworthy and Lowry.

She wrote and directed numerous plays that brought her acclaim, including her original plays:

And a Time to Dance
And the Wind Blows Free
Boy Hunter of Walpi
Boy Printer of Gutenberg
The Cabin at Medicine Spring
Feast of Raymi
Jennie
Run, Peddler, Run
Through the Perilous Night
The Twelve Days of Christmas
What So Proudly We Hail
When Satan Hops Out

Her plays *Feast of Raymi* and *The Twelve Days of Christmas* were published by Fisher Brothers.[182] After Charlotte left P-M, she headed the Children's Theatre Department and taught at the Santa Catalina School in Monterey, California, until she was ninety-two years old. Once, speeding to get to work, she was stopped by a police officer. When he asked why she was speeding, she handed him her driver's license, pointed at her age and said, "I'm running out of time."[183] When the officer found out she taught theater, he told her of his daughter, who was interested in acting.

Right: Charlotte Perry continued to teach at the Santa Catalina Children's Theatre Department until she was ninety-two years old. *Perry-Mansfield Archives.*

Below: Charlotte Perry taught her students to show not tell what a character was going through. *Perry-Mansfield Archives.*

Charlotte invited them over for dinner and ended up helping the girl get a start in acting.

Charlotte also played her Amati violin in the Monterey Symphony for twenty years, directed plays at the Cherry Foundation and participated in the Cherry Foundation Symposiums on the creative approach to the arts for children. Additionally, she directed plays at the Golden Bough.[184] She also kept her ties to Steamboat Springs, contributing to the Community Theatre and "thereby also helped raise money to transform the old train depot into a theater and community center for the arts."[185] After she retired from helping Stephens's transition, Charlotte taught summer courses at Yampa Valley College in Steamboat and Western State College in Gunnison, Colorado.

She received a number of awards, including the Tajiri Award, an award created to honor deceased *Denver Post* drama editor Larry Tajiri; the Governor's Award; and an award from the first annual Perry Awards for her outstanding contribution to local theater. In 2004, she was also inducted into the Colorado Women's Hall of Fame.

In 1972, Charlotte was asked to come back to P-M to direct one more play. She chose *Man of La Mancha*, the tale of Don Quixote. The show was sold out, with people in the aisles and along the back of the room. Crowds formed outside, and the production received a standing ovation.

In 1980, Charlotte received a copy of *Dancers on Horseback*, a book written by Lucile Bogue chronicling the accomplishments and stories of the early years of Perry-Mansfield. Charlotte wrote to her: "Helen and I are so overjoyed to read the 'Dancers on Horseback.' What marvelous work you have done with it. I can hardly read it without weeping. Sometimes I miss the old life at P.M.C. Unbearably."

Two years later, Helen Smith, the glue between Charlotte and Portia, passed away. Charlotte followed a year later on October 28, 1983. At her memorial, John Roberts, a close friend and professor of music at Monterey Peninsula Community College, played and sang "The Impossible Dream" from *Man of La Mancha*.

Charlotte is quoted as once saying, "Although we had come to this wilderness to concentrate on the arts, we lived pioneers' lives." Those three women—Charlotte Perry, Portia Mansfield and Helen Smith—with their impossible dreams, with their divine madness, not only reached the stars that would have been unreachable for others but also put the sparkle in each soul that passed through their camp, teaching them how to fly, how to dream, how to be alive beautifully, how to live impossibly.

For many, Perry-Mansfield was the impossible dream come true.

AUTHOR'S NOTE

Throughout the text, I primarily refer to Perry-Mansfield Performing Arts School and Camp as P-M. The camp has been known as Rocky Mountain Dancing Camp, Perry-Mansfield Camp (PMC), Perry-Mansfield School and Camp of Stephens College and now Perry-Mansfield Performing Arts School and Camp. My choice to use P-M pays homage to the notion that Helen Smith, an integral part of Perry-Mansfield, was considered the dash between Charlotte and Portia, or the glue that held them together.

P-M has been many things to many people over the years. In this book, I have tried to capture the essence of P-M through the camp's major accomplishments. There are many, many people who have

Helen Smith was the dash in Perry-Mansfield and the glue that held the ladies together. *Perry-Mansfield Archives.*

had a profound influence on P-M who are not mentioned in this book due to space restraints. That does not, however, negate the important contributions they made at camp.

NOTES

Introduction

1. Perry, interview with the author, August 2014.
2. Charlotte Perry and Portia Mansfield, interview with Lucile Bogue.
3. Ibid.
4. Ibid.
5. Ibid.
6. Scrapbook clipping, New York Public Library for the Performing Arts, Dorothy and Lewis B. Cullman Center.
7. Perry and Mansfield, interview.
8. Ibid.
9. Delsarte Project, "Brief History of Delsarte."
10. Ibid.
11. Perry and Mansfield, interview.
12. Ibid.
13. Ibid.
14. Ibid.
15. Pam Wheaton, "Charlotte Perry: Grand Lady of Theatre." *Steamboat Pilot*, September 18, 1975.
16. Ibid.
17. Ibid.
18. Ibid.
19. Ingrid Wekerle, PhD, interview.

Chapter 1

20. Rocky Mountain Dancing Camp brochure, 1913, Perry-Mansfield Archives.
21. Reed, "Annie Dickinson Brown."
22. *Denver Post*, August 28, 1915.
23. Ibid.
24. *Herald Weekend Magazine*, June 22, 1975.
25. Charlotte Perry, "Perry-Mansfield: Haven for the Arts in the Rockies. Part One: Our First Ten Years," *Pine Bark*, Perry-Mansfield archives.
26. Ibid.
27. Ibid.
28. *Routt County Sentinel*, July 21, 1916, Colorado Historic Newspapers Collection, Colorado State Library.
29. Perry, "Perry-Mansfield."
30. Ibid.
31. Perry and Mansfield, interview.
32. Perry, "Perry-Mansfield."
33. "A Most Unusual and Complete Department—Under the Direction of Marjorie Perry Assisted by Frances Hartsook," Perry-Mansfield brochure, 1915, Perry-Mansfield Archives.
34. Ibid.
35. DeLucia, interview with the author, July 2016.
36. *Routt County Sentinel*, July 21, 1916.
37. Perry and Mansfield, interview.
38. *Steamboat Pilot*, July 3, 1918.
39. *Routt County Sentinel* March 22, 1918.
40. Ibid., July 5, 1918.
41. Rocky Mountain Dancing Camp brochure, 1918, Perry-Mansfield Archives.
42. *Routt County Sentinel*, "Attendance at Dancing Camp Breaks All Records," July 18, 1919.
43. Lillian Von Qualen, "The Saga of Steamboat Springs: The Perry Mansfield Camp School Has Lived Through a Generation of American Dance," *Dance Observer* (June–July 1939).
44. *Routt County Sentinel*, August 22, 1919.
45. Rocky Mountain Dancing Camp brochure, 1920, Perry-Mansfield Archives.
46. *Pine Bark*, 1920.

47. Perry and Mansfield, interview.
48. *San Francisco Examiner*, "Nymphs on the Beach Lend New Delights to Carmel-by-the-Sea," 1927.
49. *Routt County Sentinel*, "Dancing Club Season on Coast Highly Successful," April 29, 1921.
50. Candace Gay Hibbard, oral history, Perry-Mansfield Archives.
51. *Routt County Sentinel*, "Dancing Camp Is Place of Beauty," June 9, 1922.
52. Ibid.
53. Ibid., August 19, 1921.
54. Ibid., "Enjoy Artistic Dances," September 3, 1920.
55. Ibid., September 2, 1921.

Chapter 2

56. Jeanne Fuller, interview with Lucile Bogue.
57. Mary Ann Mansfield, wife of Malcolm B. Mansfield, nephew to Virginia Mansfield, "Virginia Elizabeth Mansfield," 2000.
58. Ibid.
59. Perry and Mansfield, interview.
60. Perry, Smith and Mansfield, interview.
61. Von Qualen, "The Saga of Steamboat Springs."
62. Unnamed source, New York Public Library for the Performing Arts, Dorothy and Lewis B. Cullman Center.
63. Perry, Smith and Mansfield, interview.
64. Ibid.
65. Charlotte Perry, "The Story of Perry Mansfield: Part Two: We Take to The Road," *Pine Bark*, January 1965.
66. Ibid.
67. Ibid.
68. Ibid.
69. Perry-Mansfield brochure, 1923, Perry-Mansfield Archives.
70. Glenn Poulter (original writing), adapted for an oral performance at *The Tread of Pioneers Museum*, October 7, 1994, Rusty DeLucia collection. During the Depression, Eleanor was asked to run her father's business. She got her broker's license in 1932 and worked for a large real estate firm. During World War II, she was offered a job as the executive secretary for the all-male Explorer's Club. The club had to change bylaws to let a woman work there. When her parents died in 1948, she moved back to

Steamboat Springs, where she established a one-woman real estate and insurance office in Denver during the winter and in Steamboat Springs in the summer. Eleanor headed the committee to renovate the old train depot, which is now home to the Steamboat Springs Arts Council.

71. *Steamboat Pilot*, July 1, 1925.
72. Portia Mansfield's journal, Perry-Mansfield Collection, History Colorado, Stephen H. Hart Library and Research Center.
73. *Routt County Sentinel*, "To Have Theatre at Dancing Camp," March 13, 1925.
74. Ibid., "Dancing Camp to Be Open One Day," June 19, 1925.
75. Perry-Mansfield brochure, 1925, Perry-Mansfield Archives.
76. Perry-Mansfield songbook from the mid-1920s, Perry-Mansfield Archives.
77. Perry and Mansfield, interview.
78. *Steamboat Pilot*, "Final Show at P-M Camp on Tuesday," August 23, 1929.
79. Perry and Mansfield, interview.
80. *Steamboat Pilot*, August 10, 1927.
81. Perry-Mansfield brochure, 1929, Perry-Mansfield Archives.
82. Ibid., 1928.
83. *Steamboat Pilot*, "New Division of Perry Mansfield: Miss Mansfield Announces Establishment of Recreative Camp for Women—Here to Prepare for Summer," May 31, 1929.
84. Perry-Mansfield brochure, 1929, Perry-Mansfield Archives.
85. *Smith College Quarterly*, 1929.
86. Equestrian Coach, "Captain Vladimir S. Littauer."
87. Letter from Charlotte Perry to Lottie Perry, Marjorie Perry Collection, Denver Public Library, Western History.
88. Perry-Mansfield brochure, Perry-Mansfield Archives.

Chapter 3

89. Mansfield, interview with Lucile Bogue.
90. Charlotte's speech on correctives, Perry-Mansfield Archives.
91. *Steamboat Pilot*, "Camp Will Open July 1 with New Features and with a Large Faculty of Instructors," June 17, 1932.
92. Perry-Mansfield brochure, 1932, Colorado Historic Newspapers Collection, Colorado State Library.
93. Ibid.
94. *New York Sun*, "Dance Away Ugly Moood," March 30, 1931.

Chapter 4

95. Perry, interview.

96. Historytogo.utah.gov.

97. *Steamboat Pilot*, "Novel Party Was Enjoyed: Faculty and Students at Dancing Camp Had Progressive Banquet—Work Is Getting Well Under Way for Summer," July 15, 1932.

98. Marianne Crowder's recollections of camp, Perry-Mansfield Archives.

99. *Steamboat Pilot*, June 16, 1933, Colorado Historic Newspapers Collection, Colorado State Library.

100. Ibid., July 27, 1934, Colorado Historic Newspapers Collection, Colorado State Library.

101. Perry, interview.

102. *Steamboat Pilot*, "First Production Perry-Mansfield," August 2, 1935.

103. Perry, interview.

104. Ibid.

105. Harriette Ann Gray, interview with Lucile Bogue.

106. Kay Uemura, interview with author, November 16, 2013.

107. Perry, interview.

108. Perry-Mansfield brochure, 1936, Perry-Mansfield Collection, Denver Public Library Western History.

109. *Steamboat Pilot*, "Perry-Mansfield Directors Are to Teach in New York," September 16, 1937.

Chapter 5

110. Lillian Von Qualen, "Barnstorming in the Rockies," *Dance Observer* (May 1940), 64.

111. Ibid.

112. *Steamboat Pilot*, "Perry-Mansfield Performance for Red Cross Will Be Held in School Auditorium," August 8, 1940.

Chapter 6

113. *Steamboat Pilot*, "P.M.C. News," June 20, 1940.

114. *Pelham Sun*, March 31, 1955.

115. *Steamboat Pilot*, February 13, 1941.

116. Perry-Mansfield brochure, Perry-Mansfield Archives.
117. Perry-Mansfield brochure, New York Public Library for the Performing Arts, Dorothy and Lewis B. Cullman Center.
118. Harris, interview with Lucile Bogue.
119. Lillian Von Qualen, "The Burning of Clan House," Perry-Mansfield Archives.
120. Nancy L. Parker, "Where War Work Is Play!" 1943, Perry-Mansfield Archives.
121. Jed Distler, "Cage, Four Walls, Etc.," Classics Today, http://www.classicstoday.com/review/review-9466.

Chapter 7

122. *Steamboat Pilot*, "Frank Carroll Goes to Perry-Mansfield Camp," June 1938.
123. Ibid., "Guests Arrive to Receive Instruction at Well Known Summer Camp," July 7, 1933.
124. Perry-Mansfield School of Horsemanship brochure, Perry-Mansfield Archives.
125. Margery and Portia Mansfield, "Horsemanship Goes Forward," *Horse Magazine*, n.d.
126. Lillian Von Qualen, "Horsemanship in the High Rockies," Perry-Mansfield Archives.
127. Martine Richards Minnis, remembrances, 2012, Perry-Mansfield Archives.
128. Ibid.
129. Barker, interview with author, September 2016.

Chapter 8

130. Sternhagen, interview with Lucile Bogue.
131. Letter from Charlotte Perry to Lottie Perry, Marjorie Perry Collection, Denver Public Library Western History.
132. *Steamboat Pilot*, "Perry-Mansfield Camp Will Open for 32nd Year on July 3," June 26, 1947.
133. Ibid., "Perry-Mansfield Production Is Original with Splendid Cast," August 14, 1947.
134. *Satan Hops Out*, an original play by Charlotte Perry.
135. Perry and Mansfield, interview.

136. Ibid.
137. Ibid.

Chapter 9

138. *Pine Bark*, 1951, Perry-Mansfield Archives.
139. *Steamboat Pilot*, "10th Annual Square Dance Festival in Steamboat Friday and Saturday," July 30, 1959.

Chapter 10

140. *Steamboat Pilot*, July 26, 1951.
141. Mansfield, interview.
142. Perry, Smith and Mansfield, interview.
143. Portia Mansfield's thesis on the Conchero Dancers.
144. Speech given by Ingrid Wekerle, PhD, on Charlotte Perry's passing, Rusty DeLucia Collection.
145. *Rocky Mountain News*, August 22, 1955.
146. *Steamboat Pilot*, June 7, 1956.
147. *Denver Post*, July 28, 1957.
148. *Steamboat Pilot*, "Eight Bills in Six Weeks Will Feature Theatre Festival Here: Two World Premiers," April 10, 1958.
149. *Pine Bark*, 1958, Perry-Mansfield Archives.
150. Len Aitken, *A Divine Madness*, an original film.
151. Ibid.

Chapter 11

152. Portia Mansfield, "Symposium of Arts for the Rocky Mountain Region," Perry-Mansfield Archives.
153. *Steamboat Pilot*, "Symposium of the Arts Will Begin at Perry-Mansfield Camp Saturday: Perry-Mansfield to Present First Opera in Steamboat," August 21, 1952.
154. Mansfield, "Symposium of Arts for the Rocky Mountain Region."
155. *Steamboat Pilot*, "Widely Known Arts Leaders Will Participate in 4th Symposium at Perry-Mansfield Aug. 26–28," August 4, 1955, Colorado Historic Newspapers Collection, Colorado State Library.

156. Mansfield, "Symposium of Arts for the Rocky Mountain Region."

Chapter 12

157. *Steamboat Pilot*, "Louis Horst Studio of Dance Is Dedicated at Perry-Mansfield Sunday," August 11, 1960.
158. Uemura, interview.
159. Faulkner, interview for Denver University.
160. Perry and Mansfield, interview.
161. Charlotte Perry, "Reminiscences and Plans," reprinted from *Dance Magazine*, April 1963.
162. *Pine Bark*, 1954, Perry-Mansfield Archives.

Chapter 13

163. *Steamboat Pilot*, "Perry-Mansfield to Celebrate 50th Season," March 14, 1963.
164. Mansfield, interview.
165. Harrington, interview, Perry-Mansfield Archives.
166. Henderson, interview with Lucile Bogue.
167. Stephens files, Perry-Mansfield Archives.
168. *Steamboat Pilot*, July 12, 1990.

Chapter 14

169. Clippings from Perry-Mansfield Archives.
170. Bruce, interview for Denver University.
171. Roach, interview with author.
172. http://historycolorado.tumblr.com/post/115243501805/charlotte-perry-portia-mansfield-a-colorado.
173. Wonderbound, "Sarah Tallman."
174. Roach, interview.
175. Ibid.
176. Ibid.
177. Lazarus, interview, October 23, 1913.

Chapter 15

178. *Denver Times*, August 28, 1915, Perry-Mansfield Archives.

179. Perry, interview.

180. From the Perry-Mansfield Boys' Camp Scrapbook, 1969 History Colorado, Stephen H. Hart Library and Research Center.

181. Charlotte Perry to Carol Gossard, History Colorado, Stephen H. Hart Library and Research Center.

182. Wekerle, speech.

183. Wekerle, interview, for Denver University.

184. "Co-Founder of Perry-Mansfield School of Theatre and Dance Miss Charlotte Perry Retires," Rusty DeLucia Collection.

185. Wekerle, speech.

BIBLIOGRAPHY

Books

Anderson, Daisy. *From Slavery to Affluence: Memoirs of Robert Anderson, Ex-Slave*. Steamboat Springs, CO: Steamboat Pilot, 1967.

Bogue, Lucile. *Dancers on Horseback*. San Francisco: Strawberry Hill Press, 1984.

De Mille, Agnes, and Joan Acocella. *Dance to the Piper*. New York: NYRB Classics, 2015.

Duncan, Isadora. *My Life*. New York: Liveright, 1996.

Lefevre, Camille. *The Dance Bible. The Complete Resource for Aspiring Dancers*. Hauppauge, NY: Barron's Educational Series, 2012.

Limoli, Denise Warner. *Dance in Saratoga Springs*. Charleston, SC: The History Press, 2013.

Reed, Leda. "Annie Dickinson Brown." In *Historic Boulder Park: Yesterday and Today*, ed. Leda Reed, Charles H. Toll, Katharine Wolcott Toll and John Quincy Adams Rollins. N.p.: n.d.

Williams, Rita. *If the Creek Don't Rise*. Orlando, FL: Harcourt, 2007.

Institutions

Denver Public Library Western History

History Colorado, Stephen H. Hart Library and Research Center

Perry-Mansfield Archives

New York Public Library for the Performing Arts, Dorothy and Lewis B. Cullman Center

Interviews

Barker, Naomi. Interview with the author. September 2016.

Bruce, Michael Kelly. Interview, Denver University, Carson Brierly Giffin Dance Library.

DeLucia, Rusty. Interview with the author. July 2016.

Faulkner, T. Ray. Interview, Denver University, Carson Brierly Giffin Dance Library.

Fuller, Jeanne. Interview with Lucile Bogue. Perry-Mansfield Collection of History Colorado's Stephen H. Hart Library and Research Center.

Gray, Harriette Ann. Interview with Lucile Bogue. Perry-Mansfield Collection of History Colorado's Stephen H. Hart Library and Research Center.

Harrington, Chuck. Interview. Perry-Mansfield Archives.

Harris, Julie. Interview with Lucile Bogue. Perry-Mansfield Collection of History Colorado's Stephen H. Hart Library and Research Center.

Henderson, Kay. Interview with Lucile Bogue. Perry-Mansfield Collection of History Colorado's Stephen H. Hart Library and Research Center.

Lazarus, Joan. Interview. October 23, 1913.

Mansfield, Portia. Interview with Lucile Bogue. Perry-Mansfield Collection of History Colorado's Stephen H. Hart Library and Research Center.

Perry, Ann. Interview with the author. August 2014.

Perry, Charlotte, and Portia Mansfield. Interview with Lucile Bogue. Perry-Mansfield Collection of History Colorado's Stephen H. Hart Library and Research Center.

Perry, Charlotte, Helen Smith and Portia Mansfield. Interview with Lucile Bogue. Perry-Mansfield Collection of History Colorado's Stephen H. Hart Library and Research Center.

Roach, Bruce. Interview with the author, September 2016.

Sternhagen, Frances. Interview with Lucile Bogue. Perry-Mansfield Collection of History Colorado's Stephen H. Hart Library and Research Center.

Uemura, Kay. Interview with the author. November 16, 2013.

Wekerle, Ingrid, PhD. Interview, Denver University, Carson Brierly Giffin Dance Library.

Websites

Delsarte Project. "A Brief History of Delsarte." http://www.delsarteproject. com/?A_Brief_History_of_Delsarte.

Distler, Jed. "Cage, Four Walls, Etc." Classics Today, http://www. classicstoday.com/review/review-9466.

Equestrian Coach. "Captain Vladimir S. Littauer." http://www. equestriancoach.com/content/captain-vladimir-s-littauer.

historycolorado.org

historytogo.utah.gov

perrymansfield.org

Wells, Kathryn. "Annette Kellerman—The Modern Swimmer for the Modern Woman." Last modified November 17, 2013. http://www. australia.gov.au/about-australia/australian-story/annette-kellerman.

Wonderbound. "Sarah Tallman." http://wonderbound.com/people/ sarah-tallman.

INDEX

ABOUT THE AUTHOR

Dagny McKinley has an MFA from Naropa University and a BA from the University of Western Ontario. She has lived in Steamboat Springs for twelve years, where her writings and research have focused on local histories, as well as fiction set in nature. The inspiration for this book began when McKinley saw an image of Portia Mansfield and Charlotte Perry dancing. The women appeared to be filled with such joy that she felt pulled to find out more about them. Four years and hundreds of pages of research later, this book was written.